All In For Love

All In For Love

a spiritual adventure

Lesley S. King

Copyright © 2016 Lesley S. King
All rights reserved.

ISBN-13: 9780997153101
ISBN-10: 0997153105
Library of Congress Control Number: 2015921133
Inner Adventure Books, Santa Fe, NM

*To my spiritual teacher, Sri Gary Olsen,
who guides the way inward.*

Praise for
All In for Love

"I can't express how much I enjoyed this book. Countless times in my reading I would see exact reflections of what was going on in my own life. It often brought me to tears as Lesley S. King, in subtle humility, and in sweet partnership with her dear Friend, pointed to resolutions I had not seen. The book became very personal to me, and my sense is it will become deeply personal to everyone who reads it."

—RUDY ANDERSON, EDUCATION SPECIALIST

"Reading *All In for Love* has stirred something in me, some inner questioning of my own relationship to the great river of all that is. While reading, I kept feeling a little high, a little zoned out, just like I feel after a massage. This book is a massage for the soul."

—LOIS GILBERT, AUTHOR OF *RIVER OF SUMMER*, *WITHOUT MERCY*, *RETURNING TO TAOS*, AND *LOST IN THE GILA*

"All In for Love is a gentle and sublime journey that describes meeting and embracing a perfect Master. In relating such profundity, Lesley S. King takes the reader with her, from mundane to sacred, from external to the inner reality of living in a much finer and more elevated truth. Her experiences of transcending challenging events exactly describe the simplicity of the Master's teachings, and how those teachings can be applied and then lived on a practical level. One must live the truth, not just know of it, and this book is a beautiful narrative of living and loving that others may find inspiring to accomplish the same."

—Michael Hock, substance and mental health system designer, poet, and author of *The Sky Is Walking on the Earth*

"What happens when life opens a door and you walk through it? Lesley S. King shares a universal story in her own unique voice about the spiritual journey she undertakes when one life path ends and a new one begins. King's writing soars on wings of love as new insights deepen her daily experiences. The reader is not only included but profoundly inspired."

—Allison Rand, book enthusiast and world adventurer

"Lesley S. King's spiritual journey and her most beautiful account of it are a true inspiration and a welcomed signpost on the path home. Lesley's sensitive and sincere narrative of her experience is pure gift—a beautiful example of channeled love and grace."

—Lynne McCarthy, ceramic artist, poet, and photographer

Also by
Lesley S. King

The Baby Pact, a novel

King of the Road: Adventures Along New Mexico's Friendly Byways

By the Way: A Guide to New Mexico's 25 Scenic Byways

Frommer's Great Outdoor Guide to Arizona & New Mexico

Frommer's New Mexico, Editions 5–11

New Mexico for Dummies, First Edition

Dream Vacations, Anthologized Essay: The Native American Trail

Table of Contents

Praise for All In for Love · vii
Acknowledgments · xvii

Part I   Calamity Turns Aside · 1
Eternity at Acoma · 3
Calamity Turns Aside · 7
What Have I Got to Lose? · 13
My Destination Is Now · 15
Be Lost to Be Found · 18
The Song of the Rainbird · 21
My Bully Neighbor Is Me · 24
I Love to Pay the Plumber · 28
My Mother Is Not My Mother · · · · · · · · · · · · · · · · · · · 30
Trust the Rainbow · 32
Divine Horsepower · 34
Monday in the Ocean of Love and Mercy · · · · · · · · · · · · · 36
Awaken in Soul · 38
Find Your Inner Wine · 42
Leap off the Cliff · 45
You Know You're a Spiritual Warrior When… · · · · · · · · · · 49
Plunge into the Unknown · 51

Running Waterfalls · 54
We Are Gladiators · 57
My Beloved Stands before Me · 60
Love Energy · 62
The Divine Symphony · 65
Meeting My Master · 67
Slay Your Illusions · 72
All In · 76

Part II Sustained by Love · 79
The Eternal Flame · 81
The Master Within · 84
The Lone Hatchling · 86
Be the Current · 89
Good-bye, Gloom; Hello, Radiance · · · · · · · · · · · · · · · · 90
Soul for President · 94
Where There's a Hill, There's a Way · · · · · · · · · · · · · · · 96
Launch In · 99
God's Triple-Tiered Love Cake with Ecstasy Icing · · · · · · 102
Birth of a Dream · 105
Unconditional Love · 108
Bear the Love · 109
Diamonds Aren't Forever but Love Is · · · · · · · · · · · · · · 111
The "Hell Yes" Test · 115
How to Travel Home · 117
I Am the Creator · 118
Let the War Rage · 121
Game On · 123
Scrooge Buys a Tree · 126

Waltz with the Master · 129
The Beloved's Playlist · 132
The Divine Court · 135
Road to Freedom · 140
Make the Mind Your Friend · 141
The Lover's Breath · 144
Sustained by Love · 147
Forgive Your Vanity · 151
Own Your Power · 155
The Sky of Love · 158
The Soul Emergency · 160

Part III All Is Thee Whispering to Me How to Be Love · · 165
No Matter · 167
All Exists Now · 169
Soul's Great Gear · 170
Be the Harmony You Want to See
in the World · 171
Dive Soul-First into Love · 175
Streaming Love · 176
The Stunning Higher View · 180
The Pure House · 183
Live Your Dream · 185
The Beloved's House · 188
All Is a Love Song · 192
I Am the Child · 195
Land of Eternal Radiance · 198
Dwell in Love · 199
The Great Oneness · 203

No Identity but Love · 204
I Will Always Want You · 207
How to Live Forever · 209
Harmony of the Whole · 212
When Seasons Collide · 215
The Lover Appears · 216
Life with a True Master · 219
Sounderella · 223
The Highest Quest · 225
About the Author · 229

Acknowledgments

Years ago I used to write in the cold. I thought it had to be a solitary experience, though I admired people who had communities around their creativity. Now, thanks to the Beloved, my writing feels as though it is not even mine. It flows through me while I merely hold the pen, and then it is nurtured by many. My spiritual teacher Sri Gary Olsen eased me into this new life by showing me that all is a reflection of the inner and that my job is to focus there.

My brilliant team of beta readers helped refine the book: Rudy Anderson, Lois Gilbert, Allison Rand, Michael Hock, and Lynne McCarthy. Also thanks for the encouragement and expanded viewpoints from my Inner Adventure Blog readers, commenters, and sharers, and my close friends, including Julie Zimber, Lori Goetz, Colleen Buchanan, Karen Swift, Logan Jo'el, Karina Silver, Ross Barrable, Sheila Burns, Debra Kuszewski, Al Medina, Bobby Griffith, Deborah Harvey, Jamie Pitts, Michael Baggetta, Dan Gerry, Kelley Kieve, Marian Royal

Vigil, Chloe Kyle, Sherri Ohnemus, Sagar Das, Gil Garduño, Diane Hart Tuck, Susan Stoffer, and many more.

A number of people contributed in concrete ways, helping me manifest a new life as a blogger and indie author: most notably my blogging and Internet business coaches Jane Friedman, Steve Harrison, and Brian Edmondson, and my webmaster Canton Becker.

And finally, thanks to my family, who love and support me year after year, no matter what.

PART I

CALAMITY TURNS ASIDE

—Rumi

Eternity at Acoma

I reach out my hand to move a priceless Acoma pot, and it crumbles between my fingers. In a little adobe home that sits 370 feet high atop Acoma mesa, I'm videotaping a potter who works before me coiling graceful vessels for which he is renowned. Little do I know that this broken pot is a harbinger of what, within the next few years, will happen to my life.

Stunned by my clumsiness, I step back. I had no idea an unfired pot was so fragile. I call on the Beloved and realize that I had completely lost myself in my work, something that often happens when I'm on assignment as I am now for *New Mexico Magazine.* The potter's face drains of color as we both stare at the artistry that took him days to complete—destroyed.

In this little house that smells of aged mud and dry corn, I feel weariness deep in my bones. For eighteen years I have gratefully run all over New Mexico on assignments like this, interviewing artists, photographing rodeos, and eating enchiladas. For other publications I have traveled the world; I stayed at a villa in Tuscany, an ecolodge in Costa Rica, and a Bedouin tent in Israel. I have cooked with a world-renowned chef in Provence and ridden a camel in the Negev.

And now, I am tired. My body is giving out. When I began this job, I was hearty and young. Now I suffer from food allergies and insomnia. My dream job has turned into a nightmare.

I have known this for a few years but been unwilling to let go. My ego enjoys being King of the Road, the name of my *New Mexico Magazine* column. It thrives on the power of reviewing restaurants and inns for Frommer's travel guides. And my heart adores the freedom of taking off on an adventure, leaving the weighty parts of my life behind.

But most of all, I am afraid to change. I don't know what else I might write about. I fear this is the only way I can make a living, and so month after month, I cling to this job.

Today, I woke with a headache from last night's Navajo taco. My actions and thoughts on this mesa top have been sluggish, as I've hiked along narrow streets that open to spectacular views of distant buttes and mountains. With a heavy heart, I wandered through the San Esteban del Rey Mission, built in 1640, and I listened to my guide talk of the thirteen families who still live in this ancient place they call Sky City.

As the potter and I walk to the edge of the mesa, he tries to console me. "It's okay," he says. "These things happen." But I can feel a huge shift in the energy between us, a distrust, a closing down.

I apologize again and promise to pay for the pot. He points to stairs chiseled in stone. On shaking feet, I make my way down.

In the Acoma Cultural Center at the Yaaká Café, I order lunch. I'd looked forward to this moment, staring out toward the mesa while savoring traditional Acoma food. But the red-chile posole, lamb sandwich, and horno-roasted corn sit uneaten before me.

My employer won't pay for the pot, and so I calculate the cost and realize that all of my earnings for this trip will go toward reimbursing the potter. I ask the Beloved to help me reconcile this mistake.

I see that my sadness stretches far beyond this experience. For me the broken pot is a symbol of the imminent dissolution of what has been the center of my life for almost two decades. It has been the mate that I never found, the child I never birthed. Without this job, I'm not sure I would even know who I am.

Yes, I have friends. One of the most dear is my mother who used to accompany me on these journeys, but no longer does because her health is failing. That is another part of my life: I care for her. But my work has been my true north, and now, like the pot, it is disintegrating.

From the café, I look out at the mesa and remember what I read on a plaque this morning: "Legend describes Acoma as a place that always was." I sit back and realize that though the pot—symbolizing hard work and timeless beauty—is broken, it is just a material thing. Thousands of pots have served these people and busted to pieces, and likely thousands more will too.

My true "mistake" today was not breaking the pot. Instead, it was falling asleep. I let go of my Beloved's hand. I was more concerned about the material job than preserving my connection with my inner self. I now recognize that the love and fulfillment I seek—I have always sought—come not through anything I do, but through my connection to the Divine Current flowing through me.

I sense in this moment that I am that eternal spark of the Divine. With this knowingness, this work that I cling to so tightly seems small, inconsequential. Maybe I can trust the Beloved to provide for me a life that is more suitable to who I am. Maybe that pot that evaporated in my palm is one of the best things that ever happened to me.

With a steadier hand, I eat a spoonful of posole, and it tastes delicious.

Calamity Turns Aside

*If, like the prophet Noah, you have patience in
the distress of the flood,
Calamity turns aside, and the desire
of a thousand years comes forth.*

—Hafiz

I arrive back in Santa Fe, pull into my garage and climb out of my car. Weary from my journey to Gallup and Acoma, ready to sleep in my own bed, to once again eat the healthy food that makes me feel good, I open my front door.

I see water. Inches of water cover the floor of my great room. Sensing the crisis, I chant my word, a mantra given to me by my spiritual teacher. Its calming effect helps immediately as my shoes splash from room to room, the floor covered like a baby pool with a layer of water.

I find the source under my kitchen sink, where the water purifier has split open and now spews a steady stream. I reach back and turn off the valve. The air quiets, but my heart beats so loudly the sound fills my ears and seems to make the whole house throb with panic.

I should call someone—my mother, a friend—but I don't know whom, so I continue to chant my word as I take out a mop and begin to push the water out the doors.

It's no big deal, I tell myself. Once I get the water out, all will be fine. I can open the windows for a few days and let the house dry. But my mind goes back to that Acoma pot I broke on my trip, to the sense that my life is falling apart, and a dark dread comes over me.

Exhausted, I sleep the night in my guest bedroom, which received the least damage. The next day I call my mother. She suggests I talk to my insurance company, which I do.

In the afternoon a truck arrives, along with three big men. They pace through the house, poking a monitor into the walls to check for moisture. Next they haul in fans as tall as I am and heating units nearly as large. I slink around in an attempt to stay out of the way, while assuming the men will dry the place out in a few hours and then leave.

The team leader wields a power saw and begins cutting open the walls. He makes the incision about three feet from the floor, then rips away the drywall below and pulls out the insulation.

"What are you doing?" I ask.

"It's all saturated," he says.

The air fills with the sounds of whirling fans, grumbling heaters, and grinding power saws. Extension cords weave like a tapestry across the concrete floor. I pace from room to room, watching the men work, wondering when they will leave.

I intend to cook a healthy dinner and get a good night's sleep, but soon recognize that this project is still very much in the destruction phase, with little chance that it will resolve soon. Finally I corner the team leader and ask what I should do.

"You don't want to stay here," he says. "In the next few days the temperature will be about 110 degrees."

"Where do I go?"

"I don't know—a hotel?"

I take my phone outside and call around town, only to find that on this Indian Market weekend most rooms are booked. Finally, I find one with its price tripled at Holiday Inn Express. After the work team leaves, I load up some spiritual books, my guitar, computer, some clothes, and a few things from my kitchen and head to the motel.

During the coming week, I chant my word relentlessly, calling on the Beloved to give me strength. I am deeply attached to this house, not so much for its material value, but because it is my sanctuary. It sits in a piñon forest outside Santa Fe, with views in every direction. It is warm in winter, cool in summer. Mountain bluebirds and mourning doves visit the water pool just off my porch where I sit and watch their graceful antics. And now it is torn to pieces.

Will it ever again be whole?

When I first saw this house, I had to have it. It was a perfect home and office. I always joke that I would never commit to a man, but I did commit to this place, and so I see that many powerful lessons must come through this attachment. I know my grip on it is too tight, but I can't help it. I am in love.

My fears for the future of this house go beyond the material as well. Over the years I've struggled with chemical sensitivities. After the house is reconstructed and painted, will I even be able to inhabit it with all the new toxins?

These are the concerns that try to monopolize my consciousness. I check them with my mantra and with the omniscience of my Beloved, but in the night and at dawn, they visit me with their relentless doom.

At the house I meet the contractor that the insurance company sends. He is tall, with a bit of a belly and face creased with kind lines. He explains that he is part of a team that travels the world doing jobs such as this. Their specialty is fixing water-damaged buildings. We walk through the rooms, where my furniture is piled in the middle. We discuss the floor, which he thinks he can fix, the drywall that will be replaced. He assures me the house will be as good as new.

My sense is that all of this will take a few weeks if the workers start right away.

"How long will it take?" I ask, as we stand in the driveway.

"Not too long," he says.

I wait for a more precise answer.

"I'd say two to three months."

"What?"

"Yes, there's a lot to do and it takes time."

"Where will I live?"

He explains that the insurance company will find me a place.

Throughout our meeting, I've silently chanted my mantra, but now I lose it and with it the steadiness of the Beloved's calming presence. I frantically dial the insurance company. They start right away finding me a place to live.

The next day I check out a condo. It's nice and clean, with Santa Fe–style décor and a small balcony overlooking a courtyard. But as I drive home, I feel the familiar downward pull of allergies. The carpet there, as in many rental homes, is musty, and so by the time I reach the hotel, my head is pounding and full of fog. I know I can't live in that place.

I visit another condo the following day. Two steps in the door, I turn back, the scent of cigarette smoke so heavy even that small exposure makes my head throb.

The next morning I drive down the highway to check out another house. After a decent night's sleep and a good spiritual exercise, I feel better today, but still my mind tries to race. I'm afraid that I will again face a headache, and so I feel desolate at the prospect of finding a place to live.

Tears fill my eyes, and soon I am weeping from all that has transpired in the past weeks. I pull over and cry, lumpy tears falling on my steering wheel. When I have no tears left, a sweet calm fills me. I talk with the Beloved. I see that I have to surrender.

Dear One, I say, I am willing to sleep—to live—wherever you want me to be.

I give it all to You.

In this moment I feel the grip I've had on my house loosen. Truly, as long as I have my Beloved, I can live anywhere. I feel this deep in my core. My true home is within. This is my sanctuary.

My heart soars with freedom, a sense of flying high above the earthly plane into a vast kingdom of Love.

I start the car and drive to the townhouse that the insurance company has found for me. It's a lovely two-story place, only a few years old and just minutes from my house. It has very little mustiness and a sweet, gentle feel. From the living room, I can see the blue arc of the Sandia Mountains to the south, and on the quiet patio, finches flit in and out of a fountain. Yes, I say, I can live here, and I thank the Beloved for all of it—the flood, the homelessness, and especially the surrender.

What Have I Got to Lose?

Now, set up in the condo, I try to do my usual routine of writing for a few hours before breakfast, eating, and then sitting back down at the computer. But today my magazine assignments feel like chores, and all I want to do is crawl into the king-sized bed and sleep. The experiences of the broken pot and my flooded house seem to be telling me that I am off course.

Some deep part of me knows that it is time to create in a new way. It is time to stop running all around the globe for my work, hurting my body and losing connection with my Beloved, but I don't know what to do.

I call on that Power and then let myself relax. I lie down on the couch and nearly fall asleep. Suddenly, I feel an intensity inside me that I recognize as fear—very clearly fear of failure.

Rather than run to my computer to *do* something to quell the fear, I stay with the Divine Power and simply let the feeling be. It exhibits as a tightness in my chest and stomach, pain between my shoulder blades, and a definite push to *do* something, anything in order to run from it.

But I don't run. Instead, with the Beloved, I face it. I stand before this ephemeral but real force and do not flinch. I see that it is fear of losing my worldly life, my income, and home. But with the Beloved, I sense the part of me that is eternal, that survives no matter what. Slowly, the fear dissipates like morning fog.

The next morning, I wake with a sense of "What have I got to lose?" I really can pursue something new and nurturing. Sure, I could fail, as yesterday's fear cautioned, but so what? So I'm disgraced in front of my friends. It would only harm my ego—all my friends and family members will still love me. So what if I lose money or my house—they're just things. But the ability to live my highest and truest creation—*that* is worth the risk.

My Destination Is Now

I hunch over a conference workshop table in Philadelphia listening as the instructor talks of book marketing and brand promotion. Gently, I slap my cheeks to awaken my mind from information overload.

"My sustenance is on the line!" my mind admonishes.

I call on the Beloved.

I have signed up for a yearlong course that teaches writers how to publish and promote their own books. This summer session is the first of three in Philadelphia, another in the fall, and the last in the spring. The rest of the course is taught online and over the phone. I have some ten coaches who will be helping me with many aspects of the business of being an indie author, from an Internet specialist to a speaking coach to the main teacher, who is a marketing genius.

There's only one big problem: It seems that all of the sixty or so participants here know what they are doing—they know their subject, what they want to write about and promote.

I, however, don't have a clue. All I know is that my life continues to crumble. My physical body now reacts to any foods except vegetables and light meats. My mother who is my best friend is rapidly losing her health, and even my work has become less stable. Where once I could rely on regular writing assignments, now they seem to be drying up.

Each morning I wake with an idea. *I'll blog about travel writing and teach courses online. That's it!* Or, *I'll run travel/writing courses around the world. Yes!* But the enthusiasm for the idea dies as quickly as it arrives.

I go to dinner with a new friend. In a tiny café in Philly's historic district, we eat lamb kebabs with mint, while talking about the new direction in our lives. He tells me how he plans to be a motivational speaker, and I encourage him, as he does have a very outgoing and inspiring presence.

I talk of my struggle to find a new subject to write about. He commiserates with me, assuring me that the answers will come. But I am skeptical. For many years, I have been asking for a new direction in my work, and I'm still doing the same job I've done for twenty years.

Over a dessert of fresh fruit, I find myself talking about my spiritual path, about how it helps me come to know the God within me, and, through that, my deepest dreams and desires manifest. In this moment I feel more awake than I have this whole weekend.

"That's it!" he says. "That's your content. Look at you," he adds. "You're lit with happiness."

Suddenly my body relaxes and a deep sense of connection streams through me. My head stops spinning, and my body fills with blissful love.

A quiet voice inside me whispers, "Your content is now."

With this inner quiet, I understand that I don't have to know in advance what I will say. Each day when I connect with the Infinite One, the content will come through. I don't have to control it or plan it. I can trust in the now.

When I allow my highest viewpoint to create, it produces the most brilliant work, and *that* perfectly shapes my journey.

My only destination truly is now.

Be Lost to Be Found

The Lover is Always Getting Lost.
—Rumi

Our footsteps echo through the empty chambers of the New York City Port Authority Bus Terminal. It's late as my friend Michael and I try to find a bus to take us across the Hudson River to our hotel in Newark. Exhausted from a long day at an author's conference and a night of rich food and wine, we ride up and down escalators and ask directions from strangers and uniformed men, but end up as lost as when we began. My swirling brain searches for a solution but can't hold any thought for more than a moment. It races in fear. This is the big city, and even after all my travels, I am still a New Mexico girl.

Finally, we locate a uniformed man in a basement office who directs us to a ticket booth. We pay our money and line up with a straggly group of travelers sitting on the floor at a bus gate. We wait and wait, relieved to finally have a sense of direction. But something in me remains unsettled. I strike up a conversation with a teenage boy wearing a nose ring, who tells me that this bus is going northward in New York State, nowhere near Newark. Other travelers nearby confirm the fact. Frustrated, we abandon the gate and resume our search.

We find a sign that reads "Bus to Newark," only to end up outside the station where countless taxis breathe exhaust, red and yellow lights blurred in the darkness. We ask directions from a taxi driver, who offers to take us to Newark for a hundred bucks. We leave the chaos and head back inside where the fluorescent lights sting my eyes. We buzz around more, like bees who have lost the hive. By now I am frantic, and my head pounds from the wine.

I step away from Michael, stand with my back against a cold concrete pillar and surrender. I ask the Beloved for guidance, listening in a state of complete helplessness. At first all I hear is the noise of the city, rumbling engines, honking horns, and rambling voices, but slowly the sounds fade. My heart quiets, my head stops aching, and an easy calm fills my every cell. I stay in the silence for what seems an hour, but is likely only minutes.

When I open my eyes, an African-American woman wearing impossibly white sneakers and the desperate air of a hustler strides up and says, "You're going to Newark?"

I nod enthusiastically.

"Follow me!" she says.

I shrug at Michael, who seems to appear out of nowhere. We fall in line with her.

She leads us out a glass door to where the taxis still cough exhaust. Then she motions to a tall, disheveled man, who approaches. Michael and I stop, realizing that we may be in danger. Seeing us hesitate, our guide waves her friend away.

While I hold back, watching, Michael gingerly follows her around a corner. Again my heart clinches, as I fear that he may disappear into this void of confusion. But he steps into view and signals me to come. I round the corner and there stands a bus, in a blaze of lights, like some supernatural sleigh. We give the woman some money and climb on board.

We sit in the front seats, and soon the huge bus lumbers forward. Smiling at each other, we hug. My being settles, happy to be headed "home."

What a blessing it is to be lost, to surrender, and to be found.

The Song of the Rainbird

When I arrive back in Santa Fe, I'm ready to write. In the pink dawn, I sit in front of my computer and open up my website. I already have a blog that I set up on my travel author site. Over the past five years, I've made some five or six entries, but that's all. I didn't really understand how a blog worked, how it could help an author build an audience. But now, after my course, I have a strategy. I know that the blog will just sit there unless I let people know about it, and I do that by engaging on social media. But first, I have to write.

As I read through the few posts that are already on the blog, goose bumps form on my arms. I find that I'm already writing what I want to write. These posts are about spirituality, and I know that people have resonated with them. My mother and friends have thoroughly enjoyed them. And a few years ago, in a fit of uncertainty, I applied for a magazine editing position. The CEO of the company checked me out on my website and read the blog. She called me and offered me a job based on what she read. I didn't take the job, though, because I wanted to focus more on my own writing. Finding this on my blog seems another affirmation of the direction I'm headed.

But as I try to write, doubt freezes my fingers on the computer keys. How can I ever make a living writing about this? I get up from my desk and make breakfast. Then, still unable to write, I go for a morning walk. While I make my way down the trail, my mind wants to *rely*. It dances all about, grabbing onto possible "sources" of income.

It wants to count the savings I have in the bank and rely on that, or dwell on my next Frommer's travel guides update, hoping that will sustain me. "Yes," it says, "we can write about spirituality, but we need a scheme to make money." Marry a rich man? For a second, that thought comes into the mix.

As I traverse the piñon forest, I lovingly bring my mind back to the now, to the monsoon clouds building over the Jemez Mountains and a jackrabbit crossing the trail ahead. Though my heart beats fast in fear, the Omniscient One shows me that I only need to rely on its loving power. When I bring my attention into the now, I become like the rainbird, a mystical creature that does not drink from any puddle or pool. Instead, she opens only to the limitless sustenance coming from on high. It is always here, so I know I need never fear any lack.

By the time I arrive back at my house, I am so full of love that I have no choice but to create beauty from it. I sit down, and with my Beloved, compose the first blog post of my new creation. The words flow easily as though the Divine is dictating and all I do is jot them down.

When I drink daily of the eternal love, like the rainbird, I sing its glory, and with that flow, all that I need comes to me—and to those who hear the melody as well.

My Bully
Neighbor Is Me

I sit in a meeting at my neighbor's house. Flames crackle in the fireplace as our small community convenes in a circle. This is a friendly group—an elderly couple, a young couple, and I. And yet even within the seeming peace, my leg fidgets, my mouth is parched, and my stomach clenched.

"So," I say, "we all agree to take Dee to court."

"Yes," everyone says.

I take a deep breath and call on the Beloved.

When I arrive home, I pace around, unable to settle my heart. I'm back living in my house now where, every chance I get, I open the windows to air out the new-construction fumes. The first two weeks were an eternity of headaches and flu-like symptoms, but now all is better.

I head out on a walk, chanting my mantra, releasing the situation, and trying to focus on the moment. Bluebirds flit among the piñons, while the sun blazes orange over the Jemez Mountains. But my attention keeps returning to this dilemma. For some it might be easy, but I have a fear of court and attorneys, the time and money they cost. As the president of our well association, the duty to execute our plan falls on me.

The woman we are taking to court, whom I'll call Dee, has picked fights with each of us. Her most intense warfare, though, has surrounded a well we all share. Along with refusing to pay her well bills, she has welded a lock onto the well house so no one but she could get in, shut off other members' water, and once even tried to steal the well by reissuing it in her name. She threatens lawsuits constantly. Shortly after I moved here, her belligerence would defeat me to a point where I could barely get out of bed on mornings when I had to deal with her.

While I walk, I begin to see a great symbol in this experience. It is a fight over a well—over the source—and I see that the source of all is within me already. That is the well I need to protect, my connection with the True One. I can let go of the rest, knowing that all outcomes stem from that first cause. And so as I round the final bend in the trail and head home, I make that commitment, to protect the true well, to stay with the Beloved, and to let that power be the doer. I arrive home relatively calm, ready to take the first step.

I wake the next morning with a heaviness in my chest. My spiritual practice lifts it, but still a mass of fearful gloom sits like a raven on my shoulder. I know the only remedy for it is to chant my mantra as I do what I must do today. After breakfast, I head to the Santa Fe Magistrate Court to file the lawsuit. I fill out the papers and submit them. The clerk explains that I need to hire someone to serve the papers to Dee.

I thank the clerk and turn to leave. Immediately a woman steps forward and hands me her card, which shows her name and the title "Process Server." I thank the Divine Power for taking such good care of me. The muscular and compact woman and I sit on a bench and talk. I explain our situation, and she says that it's no problem to serve Dee because she has served her twice before. She says she will text me when the task is complete.

I feel deep appreciation in my heart for the help the Beloved offers me when I am willing to walk through my fears. I head to the pool to swim. Today I more easily focus on the moment, the cool water sluicing over my body, the tightening and releasing of my muscles. Appreciation flows in. I see how my neighbor has given greatly to me. She has come at me with anger, and I have learned over time to not engage or run from that vibration, but instead to stand steady before it, knowing that I am safe. She has also helped me detach yet further from my house. Through her help, I have learned to find safety in my true home within.

As I turn over to do backstroke, looking up at the vaulted cedar ceiling, I see that the bully vibration is part of me. My neighbor reflects my shadow, a lower, fearful version of myself. That part is belligerent, pushy, and, at the same time, a victim. I used to wake every day to its fearful voice in my head, as it urged me to work harder and push more, so that I could feel safe. But now, whenever the bully voice comes in, I release it and concentrate on the great love available in the now.

When I finish my swim, I head to the car where I find a text message waiting on my phone. The process server has completed her task. We are now headed to court. I look up and see in the distance the Sandia Mountains shining blue in the midday sun. A feeling of limitless strength fills me. I'm ready to go to court, ready to face whatever the Divine delivers, knowing all brings me closer to my true self.

I Love to Pay the Plumber

I hear it in the night, the palest noise: drip, drip, drip. Of course I know what it is—we all do—that familiar sound of a leaky faucet. It is so quiet, so benign, and yet it has the power to steal my attention and make me squirm in my bed. In its syncopated rhythm nestles at least a hundred dollars in expenses.

In the morning I rise and verify that indeed my bathtub faucet is leaking. I call my plumber, Charlie, and make an appointment for him to fix it. As I work, cook meals, take a walk and sleep, my mind returns to that leak, and when it does, I feel the discomfort of having to send money down the drain, especially during this time when my job is leaking away drip by drip, and my future is so uncertain. Each time I catch my attention dwelling there, I bring it back to the Beloved and feel my whole being calm.

When Charlie arrives and begins pulling off the faucets, the fear and dread again return. I pace the house in anticipation. What if the problem is larger than the leak? Always that possibility lurks.

But I call on the Courageous One and stop my fearful movement. I look out the window at the clear, sunny sky and feel a lightness come within my being. It is gratitude I feel for Charlie—a master plumber and kind soul. I'm also grateful that today I have the funds to pay him. When he finishes fixing the leak—that's all it was—I write the check and hand it to him. A rush of elation fills me as I recognize that in this moment I am the love flow.

I say good-bye to Charlie and head out on a walk. As I step down the trail through the piñon forest, the Beloved expands this contemplation to show me that this is my job, to each day flow love, energy, and money into my life.

I recognize that I own nothing. All in my possession—my house, car, computer, and the cash in my bank account—belongs to the Divine. I am simply using those things. I smile and a spring comes to my step as I realize that I have nothing to lose, literally, since I own nothing.

As I gaze at the sapphire sky, I see a new Lesley. Whenever called upon to pay anything, I do so with love. Whatever I am asked to give, whether love to my family, energy to work, or money to the plumber, I do so with gratitude. My true wealth is my soul—that is what I nurture. That is all that deserves my attention. And everything flows from it.

My Mother Is Not My Mother

I'm blessed with a special relationship. I have spent fifty-two years with a spectacular soul who wears the body of my mother. We have traveled the world together and survived her breast cancer, the death of her daughter (my sister), and the loss of her beloved home, our family ranch.

She has seen me through tantrums, successes, and failures in work, illnesses and the passing of my one true love (besides my Beloved), who was a dog.

I have spent a lifetime trying to protect her, from hostile men, McDonald's cheeseburgers, vodka martinis, falls, and even old age.

The truth is, I have failed at this, and I always will.

How beautiful is that.

The soul in the body of my mother is here to live her life completely, to exhaust all of her passions, to laugh, to cry unbearably, and to die.

She is not my mother. She is much more than that—a soul as large as the cosmos, with a destiny far beyond raising me and becoming my closest friend.

Trust the Rainbow

I step out the door into a bright morning, finches chirping and the air scented with dew. Despite this perfection, I am jittery, my heart heavy, afraid of the upcoming day. I'm working for a new editor who is changing the direction of the magazine where I've written a monthly column for eight years.

The editor wants the publication to be a slick travel magazine focused on what people can *do.* My writing treats that topic, but more, it is about *being* in the place itself, honoring it.

I call on the True Editor.

I walk down a winding trail through piñon forest. Suddenly I see a rainbow. Its shimmering brilliance frames the blue Sandia Mountains in the distance.

As I continue to walk, I contemplate rainbows. I see that they are miraculous because they appear real—so touchable—and yet they are completely ephemeral—dissolving as fast as they arrive. They may be the height of beauty in the material world, and yet they are illusory.

This one, in this moment, confirms the truth that what is most perfect, beautiful, and real is not what I see or do, but what I can't see, what I can only sense in my most quiet moments: That voice that tells me all is fine, and that I am safe, eternal, and loved completely.

With this understanding, my fear dissipates. If the magazine's new direction and I are not compatible—then our parting will be perfect. I don't rely on the job. I am completely sustained by the rainbow of love within.

Divine Horsepower

Recently, after watching the movie *Secretariat,* about the horse that in 1973 won the Triple Crown, I was lit with inspiration. For four decades, Secretariat held fast to his winning time. When he died, an autopsy revealed his heart was twice the size of a normal horse heart.

Besides the beautiful metaphor that such a large heart evokes—about passion and ardor—qualities he had in abundance, this amazing tale has an even deeper meaning for me.

When I consider that all in the material world is merely a reflection of the higher—of one's concept of who they are—I see that Secretariat's heart, and his ability to run with such ease, were really effects of his huge courage and winning spirit.

This superhorse *owned* his running mastership.

I can do the same every day as I face my life. I can own my Secretariat power. When I connect with the Divine Current, I am tapping into the Infinite. It is the power that hurtles the

Space Shuttle beyond earth's atmosphere, that fuels great storms such as Sandy and Katrina, and that spawns creative movements such as the Renaissance. It is the power of the ocean, the sun, the entire cosmos. And It is me.

That power can be used to criticize, to overdrink or watch too many reality TV shows. When channeled to selflessly give love, the Divinity in our lives increases exponentially.

Every moment, I can choose how to harness the amazing energy of my own double-sized heart.

Monday in the Ocean of Love and Mercy

I awaken this Monday morning with a major agenda to *get things done.* My mind has lists! Priorities! Goals! Desires! I have embarked on this new path of blogging. I'm also building a platform, which means connecting with readers on Facebook, Twitter, and Pinterest.

While I climb out of bed, I do my best to calm myself down. I sit for my reading contemplation and head into my day chanting my mantra to maintain inner peace.

As I look at my calendar to see what the week holds, a new image appears. It is of me as soul—consciousness—high above all the physical-world imperatives: I bask serenely in what the mystics call the Ocean of Love and Mercy, which is the Oneness of all. This viewpoint sees that all God's creation is love, so there is no need to rush or push.

My only job is to channel to the various parts of my life. They are really just my dream—nothing comes *from* them. All I need to do is direct a little love toward work and relationships, a bit to my home, and a sweet outpouring to my physical and emotional selves. That's it, very simple.

While the mind has a thousand goals, soul has one: to unite with the Divine Essence, to *be* the love, and to give to all creation. When I sit down at my computer to write, I hear finches chirping, feel the cool morning air laced with a thread of rain, and relish the joyful delight of freedom.

Awaken in Soul

I sit at my computer editing my novel *The Baby Pact*. My protagonist swims with her boyfriend in a river in Mexico, where she connives to betray him. I fine-tune a few verbs, making them more active, and bring in more sensory details to put my reader in that place and time with this desperate character. As I work, my heart races and my palms sweat. I call on the Beloved to help me stay in a loving state.

I've been writing this novel for ten years. I used to think that it would save me from the stressful life of a travel writer that I had created. It would be published and earn money so I could sit at home and work on my next one, relaxed and full of ease. Now my vision of novel writing is more realistic. The book won't save me, but I can complete it and send it out into the world.

Three years ago, when I had a decent draft, I hired a writing coach who taught me a great deal, far beyond what I had learned in a master's program in fiction decades ago. "It should be like a silent movie," my coach Sarah Lovett said, "in which the characters' actions *show* the story." I began to see how my characters tended to yearn for their desires more than go after them.

When I contemplated this, I saw how it was also true in my spiritual life. The Divine wanted me to see that the quest is not about ruminating over or thinking about a centered state. Instead, in every moment I am to step in to create that loving state. From this, I began engaging my mantra more, which takes me out of my head and puts me in the now. I also began using my imagination in order to create the higher states I most desire: patience, generosity, and love.

Sarah Lovett also suggested that I reconsider the number of viewpoints in the book. At the time, the story had four viewpoints from which it was told. Sarah nudged me to drop two of them because, she said, those two characters' stories weren't transformative, while the other two were.

At first I thought, "No way." I'm not going to throw away some two hundred pages that I've carefully rendered. But as I contemplated this, I came to see that Sarah was right. Over the next year, I cut out those pages and moved the necessary story points into the remaining chapters. After implementing these two huge suggestions, *The Baby Pact* was a much stronger book.

Shortly after this, I asked an editor friend, Lois Gilbert, to read my novel before I started sending it out to agents. Once she had read it, we sat out on her back porch and watched hummingbirds sip sugar water from a red feeder, their flapping wings nearly invisible. She told me she liked the book, especially the chapters with my main character, Jamie. Those chapters, Lois said, were true and heartfelt, but the ones told from the point of view of the other main character, Elena, were weaker. "They didn't hold my interest," she said.

She suggested that I drop the Elena point of view and tell the story from Jamie's viewpoint in the first person. I nodded my head, while saying to myself, "No way."

In that moment, my heart sank to my knees, and even the beauty of the hummingbirds was lost. I had hoped that Lois would adore the book, would give it her blessing. This was too much to even consider. I had already cut half the book, and now I was to cut another half? I had spent years researching Elena's passion for flamenco dance and her career as a learning specialist. I thanked Lois and went home.

After contemplating this for a few days, I decided to simply try out what Lois suggested. So I rewrote the first chapter in first person, using the "I" instead of "she." Surprisingly, the chapter sang with truth and vitality. The writing came alive. So I set about dropping the Elena chapters and putting the rest of the book into Jamie's first-person point of view. When Lois read the novel again, she cherished it.

Now as I fine-tune the novel, I see that this experience of dropping the lesser viewpoints parallels my inner journey. My spiritual teacher instructs that we have five bodies: the physical, emotional, causal, mental, and soul. Each of them wants to run the show, and one's concept of oneself determines which gains precedence. If I believe that I am just a physical being, and that my needs for wealth, house, and car are most important, then that body rules my life.

As I come to know that I am truly soul, its priorities win. Balance, patience, contentment, detachment, humility, and love then govern my days. Dropping the other viewpoints in my novel represents my movement toward soul mastery, toward truly claiming that "I am soul." The other viewpoints are still there, but they no longer dominate. Instead the "I am" holds sway.

In the stunning divine system, the Beloved teaches us through every experience. Every atom in our body reflects our inner state. That atomic state reflects into each molecule in our being, into each cell, into our organs, even into the things that surround us and, larger yet, into the entire universe. The whole system is designed just to awaken us to a broader, freer, and more expansively loving view of ourselves.

I dance in the beauty of this transformation.

Find Your Inner Wine

*The Beloved has gone completely wild—He has
poured Himself into me!
I am blissful and drunk and overflowing.*

—Hafiz

In the late afternoon in my office with warm sun shining in the window, I press the send button on my computer. The whoosh of the email taking flight sends a rush through my being. I have just completed my last travel column in an eight-year stint for *New Mexico Magazine*.

I get up from my computer and pace to the kitchen. I want to celebrate! I feel the age-old pull to party—to call a friend and head out for a night of rich food, red wine, and chocolate. I pick up my phone. But I stop and instead call on the Beloved. That Power takes me on a little journey into my past.

I grew up in a family that worshipped the great spirit of alcohol. And I did my best to devote myself to its essence. I drank plenty of Coors in high school and many margaritas in college. Then I embarked on a promising gin-and-tonic practice.

My calling was cut short, when in a brief succession in my midtwenties, I lost three loved ones. My stepfather drank too much scotch, crashed his helicopter on our family ranch, and died; one of my best friends downed too many beers, left my house, and died in a one-car accident; and my sister, on the way home from a bar, was killed by a drunk driver.

For years I reeled from the losses. I had little control over my emotions, one minute happy, the next weeping, the next angry. I realized my devotion to alcohol was misplaced, and I needed a new God.

I found one, and the One found me. As Rumi says, "What you seek is seeking you."

Of course, none of my loved ones *really* died. They just headed off on their next adventure in what my spiritual teacher, Sri Gary Olsen, calls the great Foreverness. But, at the time, I didn't know that.

My family's passion for alcohol was, of course, my passion. I would not have manifested this particular dream of a life if I weren't invested in its payoffs. My mind likes to use alcohol to celebrate and to placate and, above all, to experience its greatest love—freedom.

So today, as I hold the phone in my palm, I pause and ask the Beloved, "How would you have me celebrate?"

Immediately my body fills with radiance. All thought, all planning suspends, and I am suddenly in a complete state of celebration, better than any wine, any party, and any love that I could find in the material plane.

It is a gleaming sense of complete freedom, as though the whole world shimmers with enchantment, and I *am* that grace. More and more I am blessed to live from this place, and it is the wildest, most divinely raucous party in all existence.

Best of all, it causes no harm.

I set down the phone, lace up my walking shoes, and head out on the trail near my house. The sun sets in a blaze of pink, and I stand still to embrace it, to fully live this moment, and again I feel the swell of love.

I may drink wine and eat rich food and chocolate. But I never need to *rely* on those outer rewards for my freedom. When I am in soul, I am in constant celebration.

Leap off the Cliff

I awaken feeling good, healthy, strong—alive! I'm aware that I created this through choosing love over alcohol yesterday. I step into my day with gratitude. Again the Beloved takes me back to remind me how far I have traveled to arrive here with so much peace in my life.

When I lost my stepfather, friend, and sister to alcohol-related events, I was completely adrift. I was in graduate school, which requires an immense amount of reading, and each time I picked up a book, I would fall asleep. And yet I couldn't get a full night's sleep, so desolate did the dark make me feel. It seemed that all my sources of support had disappeared. And the losses continued.

My mother bottomed out in depression, and my fiancé betrayed our trust. I found myself with no money in the bank and struggling with an illness. One snowy winter night, I wanted nothing but to die. For the first time in my life, I called out to God for help. I didn't believe in any power but my own, but I called anyway.

Within a few days, I found myself in Arizona for a family week at a treatment center, where my mother had been admitted. The counselors there gave me an ultimatum: I could continue my miserable life as it was—drinking more wine than I should, relying too much on my mate for happiness, and staying so busy that I had no time for myself—or I could follow the simple plan they outlined.

I went into the desert and, while the sun burned scarlet on the horizon, made the choice to change.

As I tottered into my new existence, all kinds of books came into my hands, through the 12-step meetings I was attending and through counselors and friends. Like a starving waif with its first taste of food, I consumed them. I learned about codependency, the futility of controlling others, and, most importantly, the power of God. That infinite source was reprogramming my mind, which had run along calcified channels about where love comes from and what I should do with my life.

At that time, my life had a dark, cave-like atmosphere, but it began to change; the melancholia began to lift. I lived in a ratty apartment that had once been a tavern. But very quickly even that setting took on a brightness, as I met new friends and engaged with life in a new way.

Each day during this time, I turned my will over to God. I learned to suspend my thoughts from ideas about how each day, each moment, should be, and let the Divine Power determine the outcomes. I surrendered my mother's drinking and the desire to marry my fiancé. But primarily, I let go of who I thought I was.

As I became willing to emerge from my little cave of ideas, the Beloved opened for me a whole universe of opportunity. Suddenly, I had the desire to see the world—to travel, to seek adventure. I still had no money, but I found a photo of graceful pyramidal peaks in Guilin, China, which I taped to a wall in my apartment. Within six months, miraculously, I was on a boat on the Li River passing through those very hills. I had secured a teaching job in Korea that paid enough so that I could travel to China and to other parts of Asia.

My inner world had split open, and my outer became astronomical.

Most importantly, my reliance on the Divine quickened my heart. It felt dangerous, as though every morning I was leaping off a cliff and would soar through my day, caught only when I would land in bed each night, panting with the electric excitement of the unknown. Everything was new and glimmered with a shiny brilliance.

At times I cried, as past images arose in my consciousness, to be addressed with the Compassionate One. Even more, I laughed as I adventured to little temples in Korea's misty hills, to a hidden surf spot accessed through caves in Bali, and to a lion's lair while on safari in Africa. Every pore of my being glowed with life, while my devotion deepened.

As I continued my reading and contemplation, I became tuned like an instrument so that I could hear the quiet nudges of guidance. Often they would come at dawn when my mind was quiet, or after my morning practice. Sometimes, the messages went against what I thought I should do.

I heard the call to return to the United States and began applying for jobs. I was offered a college teaching position in California, but while trying to fill out the paperwork, I kept making mistakes. After hours of struggling, I put my head on the typewriter and cried. I knew I had to go back to New Mexico—the place where the pain seemed to reside. Though I didn't know it then, I would meet not only the family karma I had left behind, but also the teacher who would guide me through it.

Through our many tragedies, pleasures, and adventures, we learn to dance to the current of love, what the mystics call the Sound. This melody permeates everything but can only be contacted by those willing to follow the True Guide and give up everything to hear its sweet whisper.

Then we follow the whisper into the rarefied regions that are free of pain and heartache, because there all attachment to duality disappears. When I am resonating with this soul place, I know there is no good, or bad. My devotion to alcohol was perfect because it brought me to the Beloved. My lost loves were also perfect, because those experiences taught me to love the true Source of my joy and security.

Now in my home, as I prepare for my day, some twenty-five years since that night when I first called out to God, that dazzling sense of danger remains with me. Today, like all others, I leap off the cliff and soar with my Beloved, knowing that really I never, ever have to land.

You Know You're a Spiritual Warrior When...

- You're happy for no reason.
- Your memory is replaced by Post-it notes.
- You realize that in arguments, the fault lies not on *their* side of the street, nor on *your* side of the street. You own the whole block.
- You tell your friends you have a life-threatening illness, and they say "congratulations."
- You tell your friends you're getting a divorce, and they say "congratulations."
- Your biggest thrill takes place while you sit quietly alone in your house.
- People ask you what you've been up to lately, and you can't think of a thing, but you're certain your life is more exciting than it has ever been.

- You laugh at the *beginning* of your Beloved's jokes.
- Peace is acceptable, war has its place, but that barking dog next door has got to go!
- You've detached from work, family, and possessions, but chocolate…not so much.
- You'd rather part with money than hold onto it.
- You don't know what you ate for your last meal, but you're pretty sure of what you did in your last life, and it still gives you indigestion.

Plunge into the Unknown

*What we achieve inwardly will
change outer reality.*

—Plutarch

It's four in the morning. The world is dark as I don eye goggles and a mask in order to plunge into the unknown. No, I am not spelunking into a lava cave, nor am I diving deep into a tropical ocean, though this takes as much courage. Instead, I am plunging my kitchen sink.

Why at such an early hour, with so much determined effort?

Simply, it is time. For two days I have trusted Drano to do the job, but it failed to penetrate the murky sludge. During this time, I have asked God what this clog reflects, since I know that my outer life is a movie of my inner. All I know is that for days I have been sleepy and tired of life.

And still the clog persists.

Until this morning, when in bed, my discomfort grew so acute I could no longer ignore it.

So as I approach the sink, I see that my life is clogged.

I have a novel to publish and a new website to make live.

Though I have kayaked class IV rapids and scaled 5.10 granite faces, creating a new life most makes me shiver. The last time I recreated my life, I needed Prozac and thousands of dollars of therapy. Now, instead, I rely on the True Counselor.

So as I push the plunger up and down, the water sloshing, the acid scent of Drano filling my head, I become willing to do as Christ said: "Whoever finds his life will lose it, and whoever loses his life for my sake will find it."

I am afraid to lose my dignity through publishing this novel that was a decade in the making, and through exposing my new website to the light of the world. I fear failure.

But I have no choice. I have to take these actions. Each morning, in my spiritual practice, I commune with the Sound Current, the God essence infusing all of life. Then I step into the world and actuate that Current, and thus my outer life changes to reflect my inner.

My mind is fearful, because it doesn't know what the new picture will look like, and so it wants to create from the old ones. It wants to be the travel writer or the college writing teacher. But there is a new image that has formed instead.

It is my Beloved.

I am committed to letting my outer life stem from this image. It takes courage to live in the moment, to let the Beloved reveal my next step. This way I create from infinite soul rather than from limited mind.

With the Beloved, I planned and embarked on this amazing trip into creation. It is full of every extreme and everything in between. I can embrace it, love it, live each challenge with my whole heart. Like Ernest Shackleton, Jacques Cousteau, and Amelia Earhart, I am a fearless adventurer plunging into the unknown.

Suddenly, I hear it, a distinct sucking sound, as the drain opens and the stagnant muck rushes out.

I run water in the sink, and it flows through.

Running Waterfalls

Turquoise pools shimmer
palm trees wave
and parakeets zip by.
I paddle my kayak toward an infinity line
with nothing but blue sky beyond,
while the current pushes me into the unknown.

Headed toward the fall's lip
my fingers tremble on the paddle
my blades slice tentative strokes.
I call on the Beloved,
reach the edge and fly.

Water splatters around my head
and roars in my ears.

All In For Love

I am weightless
as I commune
with the divine buoyancy.
I have suspended all thought
and am completely in the now,
bare in its blue expanse
its airy possibility
its limitless love.

My bow pierces down
through frothy, bubbly white
and continues underwater.
Cool liquid surrounds me,
brushing my face
and penetrating my ears.
I plunge deeper,
while bubbles of insight
and inspiration percolate.

I rise back to the surface.
My whole being glows
and the world shimmers
with the sense that
nothing can stop me
in my quest for truth and love.

Reveling in a new freedom,
I head toward the next fall.

Lesley S. King

my boat a little tippy,
but I paddle forward
with yet more love.

Every moment a waterfall
en route to the great Ocean
that I am.

We Are Gladiators

What we do in life, echoes in eternity.
—Maximus in *The Gladiator*

Recently, I committed to bringing my new creations into the world—my website and novel. Since then, I have become a gladiator.

The critics have arrived to show me my foolishness, to tell me I shouldn't publish, that instead I should start again, try harder, think more. With my Beloved, I have met them face-to-face in the dust and blinding sun of the coliseum.

They appear as allies, with my best interest at heart. One suggested that I may want to start a new novel, a more spiritual one. That cut right to my core—only because that is the very criticism a voice within me has been saying for years.

If I do not recognize it inside, that criticism appears spoken aloud on the outer, by a family member, friend, colleague, or stranger.

I am grateful that it does.

I have tried to believe it. Maybe my novel should be about a woman who wants God, rather than a woman who wants a baby. Yes, I think, my critic is right. That would be a better book.

But this morning I see that they are the same. Whatever we seek is the most precious and Godly thing, whether it be a trip to the Bahamas, a baby, or God himself. It is all love. It all teaches us how to love, how to quest for the highest.

Every time I reach, every time I risk, I am grasping for God.

When I reach for something in the material world, I may get it, but with wine comes the headache, with the rose, the thorn.

However, when I seek the highest, I manifest no hangover or skin prick.

Only love.

The beauty of facing that fearful voice within is that I see how its judgment casts not only on my novel but also on my life.

Always it is there to tell me I am not spiritual enough. If I were, why would I manifest loneliness or anger? Why would I be involved in a lawsuit or struggle to sleep at night?

But these challenges are completely spiritual. They are the petals that make up the great lotus of my being. All of them, the whole of my journey, is God. To paraphrase a saying by my spiritual teacher, life is love and love is life.

I practice compassion for that part of me—and the person reflecting it—who doesn't know that all is spiritual, and we are completely loved.

Whether I publish the novel or not doesn't really matter. What is important is that I keep hold of my Loved One's hand. That simple act spiritualizes everything.

I have contacted the publisher, ready to move forward with *The Baby Pact,* a novel about a forty-year-old woman who is willing to go to any length to have a child. It is a pursuit as valid as that of Odysseus, Siddhartha, or Arjuna.

As are all adventures.

I am a gladiator, wielding my sword at the forces that conspire to stop my quest for truth. I stand tall in the center of the vast coliseum of life. While the crowds boo and cheer, while my adversary wields a spiked wrecking ball, I call on my Beloved inner self and watch as the illusion disappears, leaving me in a sweet wildflower meadow, where sunny love rays warm my smiling cheeks.

My Beloved Stands before Me

While my mind yearns to pen a
profound thought
my Beloved sits in the sink
ready to be washed.

While my mind seeks to be "liked"
in cyberspace
my Beloved stands before me
waiting to be hugged.

While my mind wants to fly away
to an exotic land
the morning dawns,
calling to be heard.

All In For Love

My Beloved is all
these hands
that give
these eyes
that see
these ears
that hear.

My Beloved is love.
My Beloved is me.

I invite you to view the video of this poem at www.lesleysk-ing.com/my-beloved-stands-before-me.

Love Energy

Today I teach a writing class. I wake with a shiver of trepidation in my spine. Yes, I am charged by the idea of giving what I know to a group of interested students convened by an organization called Wordharvest. But what overshadows that is a fear that during this all-day course, I will run out of energy.

Energy has, at times, been a challenge for me. As a child, I was beset with tonsillitis and never knew when it would swoop in and steal my strength for days. And later I found that when I lacked enthusiasm for anything—a job, a lunch date, a family gathering—I would feel as though my body were burdened with 400-pound barbells.

Of course, I would push through, do what I had to do. But I usually feared that in the midst of the experience, I would suddenly run out of gas. My body would simply give up.

In recent years, as my work as a travel writer took a toll on my health, the problem became serious. Now, I no longer work eight-hour days, and I marvel at people who do.

So the prospect of a full day of teaching and relating appears ominous this morning. As I eat breakfast, my mouth goes dry, the blueberries sticky on my tongue.

On the river, kayakers have a saying: "If you can spit, you can run it," meaning if you can spit in a rapid, it is likely not too difficult for you. If you are so afraid that you can't muster up saliva, you might want to portage your boat around the obstacles.

This morning I can't spit.

But as I put on my best blouse and slacks, as I don my work shoes, I keep bringing my attention back to the now. I release the fear and ask the Beloved for help.

Just as I walk out the door, He gives it to me.

Suddenly I see everything as energy: my car, the piñon trees, and the blue wave of the Sandia Mountains in the distance. And, most importantly, myself. I recognize that I need not concern myself with generating energy. Instead I simply keep my attention on the now, with the Omnipotence, and when I do, I am all energy.

Exhaustion comes when the mind is on the ascendant, thinking, calculating, stopping, starting. But when I am present in the now and holding my Beloved's hand, all becomes quiet, smooth, lucid, and flowing. The energy surges through me—so much that I easily give because I really have too much to contain.

As I cruise on my dirt road, I watch my mind reach forward to figure out the day—and my energy drops. But the minute I bring my attention back and focus on the Beloved, it returns. And still as I turn onto the highway, my thoughts begin to fret and plan, but I redirect them to the ribbon of pavement and blue sky before me. Each time I do, I feel the charge of the beautiful energy that I am.

The class follows in a similar way. In a cave-like room, with eight students sitting in a circle, I keep the Beloved's image before me. I'm teaching travel writing, but in a contemporary age where the writer owns more responsibility for promoting oneself. My students enthusiastically take in what I say. When I lose my focus, fear rushes in, telling me that I'm failing, that I need to try harder. I refocus, and the zeal and power return. When we finish, the students thank me and I thank the Beloved.

I am all energy, all love, a limitless flow available to take me home.

Next time, though, I'll make it a half-day course.

The Divine Symphony

I am the instrument
upon which the Divine plays
its tune of love.

I am always ready
awake
for the next pluck
of its resonance
the next puff
of its breath
the next beat of its heart.

No future note exists
nor past
only this moment's song.

Lesley S. King

I am ready, Dear One
to be the symphony
that I am.

I invite you to view the video of this poem at www.lesleysking.com/2012/06/the-divine-symphony.

Meeting My Master

A wet nose presses against my cheek and I awaken. My cat, Arjuna, snuggles into my neck. I scratch under her chin and around her jaw, feeling a bit of anxiety about the day. And yet, I also feel thrilling elation. Today I will see my spiritual teacher and hear him give a satsang—a talk—to his students.

He holds three seminars throughout the year, and today is one of them. They always fill me with bliss, but, beforehand, my mind gets a bit nervous, knowing that it will have to step aside to let Spirit flow in.

Once in a while, I'm surprised that I have a spiritual master. In Western culture it is uncommon. But when I reflect on my life, I see that every experience prepared me to meet my Beloved.

When I returned from Asia to New Mexico, I found a job teaching writing at a community college. The work was fulfilling and challenging. I also met a mate who shared many of my interests. We skied, kayaked, and biked together. We laughed with friends and spent time with our families, which were here in New Mexico.

And yet, as the novelty of this new life wore off, I once again found myself with an empty heart. In an attempt to fill it, I continued to consume spiritual literature: Shakti Gawain, Deepak Chopra, Thomas Moore, Krishnamurti, Shunryu Suzuki. Although I read and reread the uplifting works and practiced meditation each morning, I still felt empty much of the time and was unable to manifest the loving practices these writers taught. My despair was so deep that I actually plotted my demise.

I enlisted the aid of a psychiatrist who put me on Prozac. This helped me make some big changes. By this time, I had grown weary with teaching and wanted to see if I could make a living as a writer. My writing had been published in a few magazines, so my confidence was building. I also sensed I needed to leave my relationship. When I realized the outer common interests in sports and our families no longer were enough to fulfill me, I sought a deeper connection.

Aided by the antidepressant, my depression lifted, and I was able to quit my job and leave the relationship. Suddenly my life took on a new radiance. I began writing about art and events for the local paper, and about travel, food, and adventure for regional and national magazines. I wrote a series of travel/food articles for the *New York Times*. I met new friends while kayaking and began rock climbing and taking extended river trips. And then I met a man who would bring me to my knees.

It happened on a cool spring day while kayaking the Rio Grande River near Pilar. In a little, red play-boat, he dazzled my friend and me with his skills at surfing holes and playing his way through high-water rapids that I barely survived. As the sun set that evening, we stood near the river and flirted while he drank a beer and I drank water.

He was six years younger than I, and I was infatuated in a way I had never been before. In the coming years we dated, but he never really landed with me. He was always at the very edge of my fingertips as he headed off on a paragliding trip or to a new job in a new state.

Sometimes he would return my calls or be with me in a completely loving way, and sometimes I wouldn't hear from him for weeks. I knew that the love was inside me—I had read this a thousand times—and yet my heart could not stop breaking.

Meanwhile, my work that had become so enticing took on a bit more of a mundane quality. I still enjoyed the travel writing, but of course it was now a job. I had serious deadlines for magazines and for Frommer's travel guides, which was my most lucrative assignment. Once again I'd found myself with a restless and empty heart.

A friend had recently become a student of a spiritual master. When she told me, I grew fearful. "How could she trust some man with her most inner sanctity?" I wondered. To honor my discomfort, she didn't talk much of him, but she did seem to have a different viewpoint from the rest of my friends.

When I talked of my challenges with my mate, she didn't say the usual girlfriend platitudes: he's a jerk, ditch him, there are more fish in the sea. She said something completely different. Gently she would say, "You know, Lesley, you can be happy no matter what he's doing. Simply keep your attention in the moment, and each time it goes to him, bring it back. That is where the love and joy are."

I started trying this and found it worked. Then she gave me some tapes of her teacher's talks, but at first they didn't interest me. Yet one day, I put one in my car stereo and I heard, really heard, how different the message was. Rather than using the mind in an attempt to change my world and myself, as I had in past, only to end up once again back where I started, the Light and Sound teachings seemed to rely on the Divine Power to usher in change. The focus seemed to be on connecting to this Power.

I went to Albuquerque to a ballroom at a hotel to hear my friend's teacher, Sri Gary Olsen, speak. I knew that his teachings centered on the fact that the church or temple are within each of, thus he has no physical place where his students convene. Sitting in the front row, I still remained skeptical, but my heart was so empty, so at the very end of everything, that I had no choice but to listen.

The presentation began with a calming chant to settle everyone down and focus our attention. Then Sri Gary came onstage. He stood tall and lean, with a full head of golden hair and a humble but powerful presence. He didn't wear a turban or a robe, just normal dress clothing: slacks, a shirt, and a V-neck sweater.

He talked of how we are all Gods in swaddling clothes, that everything in our lives is perfectly orchestrated to help us realize this Godly state. He explained many things about our journey through the body chakras to our home in soul, where we are one with the Divine Power that creates all.

What most struck me was how I felt in that ballroom, sitting next to my friend and looking at this spiritual master. For the first time, I felt love—just a flicker of a pure and unconditional calm that didn't seem to come from outside but instead emanated from within. I felt connected to all and everyone, a certainty that everything was just fine.

When Sri Gary finished, I went out to the lobby, borrowed a piece of paper and pen, and, with a trembling hand, wrote a letter to him. In it I said, "I've come to see that I don't know where love is. It's not in my work, nor family, nor mate. I hope you can show me."

A few weeks later, I received a letter accepting me as a student of the Light and Sound teachings of MasterPath.

Now, some eighteen years later, as I pack my little bag to go spend the night at a hotel in Albuquerque, where I will once again sit before my Master, I am filled with delight. The Divine gives us everything we desire, in one way or another. Once my desire had refined enough to know that seeking outward no longer fulfilled me, the Beloved Master appeared to guide me to unimaginable glories—inside.

I pet my cat and tell her I love her, then close my suitcase, and head out the door.

Slay Your Illusions

*Seeing my friends and relatives present before me
in such a fighting spirit,
I feel the limbs of my body quivering
and my mouth drying up.*

—Arjuna, the *Bhagavad-Gita*

Today, as I look into my mother's furious eyes, I feel the temerity of Arjuna. He is the great warrior in the *Bhagavad-Gita* who must go to battle and slay his relatives, friends, and teachers.

My mother is eighty-five years old, a dear friend. I am her primary caregiver as she negotiates the perils of losing her sight and breath.

"I've already given you so much," she says to me as I sit at her bedside. "I don't see why I should also pay you."

About six months ago, when her needs increased, I asked her to pay me for the time I spend managing her household. Though she went along with this plan, she is now struggling with it. Her idea of family is that, out of a sense of duty, we go to any lengths to take care of one another.

Her anger strikes like a spear through my heart. It is true, she has given me a great deal, but I too have given to her. While she has always been a strong advocate of my writing and life path, I helped her through cancer, addiction, and grief.

So as I sit across from her and look at the fire in her eyes, I shiver.

In this moment, I am slaying the concept of family love.

I call on the Divine and ask why this came up. I see that a part of me is also uncomfortable with the arrangement. Although she can afford to pay me, the notion goes against my concept of what a dutiful daughter should be.

It is time to pull out my bow and arrow.

"Mom," I say. "I love you and cherish the time we spend together [for which she doesn't pay me]. But if you don't pay me, I will have to take on more work, and my life and health will be challenged. This job of managing your caregivers and repairs on your house is a part-time job that cuts into my work time. It helps me to be compensated."

There have been times—many—when I gladly sacrificed all harmony and my connection to God, in order to help my family. That is no longer the case. I now know that in order to give love, I have to give to myself first.

"But what if I run out of money to live?" she pleads with me. I recognize how scary that must be, especially for someone who has never generated her own income. She raised three kids and helped two husbands manifest success, but never knew the power of generating her own earnings. Now she relies on savings and a monthly check from our family hardware store, run by my brother.

"I see how scary that must be," I say. "But the company provides you with good income, and that's not likely going to change."

My mother nods, as though taking in what I'm saying. She knows more than anyone how my health suffers when I am under stress. Slowly, the angry crease leaves her brow, and she once again looks lovingly upon me with her deep blue eyes.

We are all Arjunas, poised at the edge of a battlefield. Our job is to take the Beloved's hand, wield our bows and arrows, and slay these illusions that we hold most dear.

In the *Bhagavad-Gita,* Arjuna says, "My infallible One, my illusion is now gone. I have regained my memory by your mercy, and I am now firm and free from doubt and am prepared to act according to your instructions."

Family itself is an illusion. In truth, as I wrote before, my mother is not my mother. She is really a soul with whom I share karma.

> We are all souls,
> nothing but the essence of the divine ocean.
> Only upon illusion's grave can we be free.

All In For Love

> When we are graced with this freedom
> a funny thing happens:
> We can fully enjoy life.
> All transmutes into love.

I cook my mother our favorite breakfast of fried eggs, potatoes, and greens. As we eat, we watch a movie and laugh.

All In

I'm all in, calling out your name,
Even if I lose the game.
I'm all in, I'm all in for life.

—Lifehouse

I open the email from an acquaintance on Facebook. This notable photographer says he has a project he'd like to discuss with me. My heart flutters with the sense of possibility. We set up a meeting for tea.

It has been a year since all of my writing work ceased to nourish me, and in that time, I have either left it or it left me. Recently I was graced with an image of myself as an unconditionally shining sun. I see that I need to switch my reliance for sustenance from the outside to the inside. Rather than lean on writing and publishers, I must rely on the True Publisher of all.

With that image leading me, I have created The Inner Adventure, where I have been blogging in earnest. I have endured many sleepless nights. During the day my fingers often tremble on the computer keys. Meanwhile, much redirection has come. I have learned that I must be as sincere as possible. When I am not, noise results—criticism and arguing from readers. And I have learned my task as a channel for the Divine is to share my experience, rather than teach.

I've invested money and time in each post. And I set about publishing my novel *The Baby Pact*. Meanwhile, I've done whatever work came my way. I've taught writing, helped my elderly mother, and written small articles for magazines.

My income has not covered the expenses, so I've cashed in some of my retirement savings to keep going.

I continue to ask for guidance.

The Inner Adventure blog touches people and helps them move more deeply into their spiritual paths, which is my goal—and so I feel success.

It also aids me. As I write each post, I listen over a period of days or weeks to the divine flow—and my understanding deepens. I claim yet more of the strength of that unconditional sun, the originator, shining onto all.

The photographer and I sit in the coffee shop and exchange pleasantries, speaking loud above the rumble of voices and the beat of too-loud punk music. He explains that he has read my travel writing and recently my blog. I tell him how touching his images are. He pauses and sips his coffee, then looks up and smiles at me. He asks me to collaborate with him on a book for which he has a publisher.

He says he chose me because of the spiritual nature of my writing.

As we discuss the details, my body fills with gratitude, for the book, yes, but that is in the Beloved's hands. I'm really grateful for my willingness to give all to the Divine, to be "all in," to do what is in front of me each day and trust that if I pursue my work in love, the Beloved will support me.

And that Infinite One is doing just that, through the love I feel each day.

That love is like skipping down a country road.

It is like a turquoise sea upon which I float.

It stretches a smile across my face and calms my fluttering heart.

It shows me that I am eternal and completely sustained. Nothing, absolutely nothing, can harm me—ever.

I am that love.

PART II

SUSTAINED BY LOVE

The Eternal Flame

I answer the phone and hear the radio producer's voice. "Are you ready to talk to Mary on-air?"

I call on the Beloved Master. "Yes!" I say.

Over the past six months, I have been a guest on a half dozen radio shows. I have told listeners how to pack in order to sail through airport security, how to find travel bargains, and how to locate the finest destinations.

But this is different.

The *Mary Jones Show*, based in Connecticut, is about "Believing in Yourself," and is quite spiritual. In the interview, Mary asks about my past. "You had a rough time when you were young," she says. "Tell us how that affected your life."

I talk about the time in my twenties when I lost three loved ones and my world as I knew it fell apart. "I rebuilt it with spirituality," I say.

"Can you explain to us what that means?" she asks.

I tell how I started reading uplifting writings each morning in order to raise my vibration to begin the day. "Twenty-five years later, I continue this practice," I say.

Mary breaks for a commercial, and I pace around my kitchen chanting my mantra to quiet my racing heart. What's truly awesome is that my excitement is from the pleasure of channeling the love. I could take or leave the interviews I've done in which I discuss travel, but this experience of sharing my truest passion leaves me completely lit.

This is a sign for me. The elation I feel helps me know that this is where I want to put my energy. It confounds the mind that something so simple as enjoyment can guide me, but why else would God give us emotions if we aren't meant to use them to help determine what works and what doesn't?

Back on the air, Mary and I talk more about my inner journey and hers. At the end of the call, she asks if I have a book about The Inner Adventure, and I explain that I am working on one. She invites me back on the show when the book is released. And so I have a new goal now: to complete this book. That goal feels as easy, light, and gentle as writing blog posts each week.

After this opportunity to talk about The Inner Adventure, I feel the inner flame burning more brightly than ever. Of course, any outer manifestation is simply an effect of that. The more I own my true self, the more brightly the inner flame burns and the more it reflects in my life as form.

I keep burning brightly by directing my attention to the Friend.

Its power is limitless. It is the spark that initiates and sustains all.

I am that.

The Master Within

When I say "Master"
I speak of God,
not the God that finds me a good parking place
or heals a sick friend,
though it might.

This is the Power
that creates and sustains all,
that asks me to rise above pain, pleasure,
loss and gain
in order to unite with It.

My teacher, my Master,
embodies this Source
but He is simply the outer form
of a Power that is within me.

All In For Love

When I align with this Vibration
all challenges fall quickly at Its feet
without the mental and emotional gymnastics
I once knew,
leaving me free to climb
high into the branches
of Bliss.

This heaven isn't after,
but within this life.

I come to know the Masterpower
love It
and thus
be It.

The Lone Hatchling

In a nest on my porch sits a lone hatchling. I am likely responsible for the death of its siblings.

A month ago on my porch, I checked the hanging plant that last year hid a nest. But this year I didn't find one. And yet I sensed there must be one because I had seen a finch fly in and out.

With the garden hose, I watered the plant. Still the finch came, so I checked more deeply and underneath the miniature daisies found a nest. To my horror, three of the eggs were sitting in the leaves. Only one remained tucked in the nest.

My heart clenched with the sight. I assume the water I poured into the plant floated the eggs out. With a stick, I gingerly moved them back in and then I waited, hoping I hadn't interfered too much with the finches' lives.

One day a baby hatched. It was a breath of fur and pink skin, an image that made my heart leap. And then I thought maybe another egg had hatched as well. But in subsequent days, I peeked in only to find the remaining eggs unbroken.

The sight brought a similar weight of sadness that I have felt lately in conflicts with my mother.

Always, she wants more of my time. I give what I can—many hours a week—but ultimately I must disappoint her. I don't mean to, but I hurt her.

My spiritual teacher assures me that, in God's eyes, all is perfect, and when I center in divine love, I see that it is the omnipotent Creator. The life that was to fill those little eggs will flourish elsewhere. Nothing can stop the Divine from fulfilling its purpose.

Next time I will follow the quiet nudge that told me there was a nest in that plant. And that is my lesson here: To listen more attentively to the subtler reality around me.

And to stay in the divine love, where all is perfect.

I have spent my life trying to atone for the hurts—the lapses in judgment, the bursts of anger, the jealousy and greed—that I have manifested with lovers, family members, friends, and animals.

I now see that there is only one solution: give them to God.

I come into the now and live my life from the highest vibration possible. Only that movement dissipates the karma that is far too complex for me to make right—far too tight a coil for me to unwind.

What this soul in the body of my mother owes me, what I owe her—who can calculate? How could I ever fix the "mistake" of floating those precious eggs out of the nest?

I can't.

It is not up to me to balance the scales of justice. What I can do is center in my Beloved and be true to me. From that place, all balances automatically.

As Rumi says,

"You are not meant for crawling, so don't.

You have wings.

Learn to use them and fly!"

The lone hatchling?

Now he flies about my porch and beyond into the broad world.

Be the Current

As I make over my career into a more loving experience, I find myself wanting to be saved, to have some big windfall come in so that I will know that I have enough money and energy to support myself. But this morning, during my practice, I see that my windfall is right here, right now, with my Master.

Life is like a river. My fearful mind wants out of the flow. It wants to stand dry on the shore and say, whew, glad I arrived. But truly the great thrill is being *in* the flow of the river—to *be* the current, moving freely along the bank.

For the current, life is dynamic and fun, full of witty ripples, profound curves, and hilarious waves. That is my life when I unite with the Beloved in the now. When I do this, abundance comes to me exactly when I need it. The Divine doles it out in a balanced and healthy way, which continuously supports my great love flow.

Good-bye, Gloom; Hello, Radiance

*All your pain, worry, sorrow will someday apologize
and confirm they were a great lie.*

—Hafiz

I lie on the couch in my living room, the shutters drawn, while my body experiences the effects of an allergic reaction. It has taken my strength and my desire to participate in my life.

Before this happened, I was feeling stronger and closer to the Master than I ever have. My days felt easy, fueled with an unshakable inner strength.

What has taken me down?

The malaise started just days after visiting my childhood home. My mother and I went to our former ranch to see my brother and his family. A few times a year, I go to the Watrous Valley in northeastern New Mexico. It is a magical place. Truly, in this life I was blessed with a stunning home.

Once a stagecoach stop on the Santa Fe Trail, it is a huge adobe hacienda surrounded by black willows. A river where blue herons nest flows nearby, and beyond, broad plains stretch like a green ocean.

And yet, as a child, within all the beauty, I experienced colossal pain.

It was a place of war—among my parents, my sister and me, and my brother. It is the place where I experienced the loss of my stepfather and my close friend, as I spoke of earlier.

Although my family no longer owns the house where so much drama took place, my mother and I drove by it en route to my brother's, which still sits on a part of the ranch.

Our day at his home was fun and easy. I held the Beloved close as my family feasted on a lunch of salmon, accompanied by much laughter. It was the anniversary of my sister's death some thirty years ago, and although we did not speak of it, it was there as a tender spot among us.

On the way home, Mom and I encountered a severe accident on the highway. Wounded people lay on the ground, while a helicopter landed there to lift them to a hospital. The synchronicity of the sight stunned us: at age twenty-six, my sister died in a car accident.

When I arrived home, I was fine, for a few days, until my body collapsed.

In bed at night, I nurse my pained stomach, feeling the weight of my past in that house and on that land. The sadness of it seems too large to bear. It is like a tragic novel—like *Wuthering Heights* or *Jane Eyre* in its epic sorrow. The fields lie dark, and the house holds a ghostly gloom.

I call on the Master and face the sadness. I cry until my heart and belly soften, until my mind eases into a cirrus calm.

I have never really questioned those memories. They were always just tragic. But this time I meet them with the great Neutralizer, who shows me the truth.

No tragedy, none at all. In one instant that Power lifts, like a morning fog, all the gloom.

The fighting, the death—that is just the way of the lower worlds. Back then, my fellow family souls and I were simply working through our base energies. They are all about survival—fighting for life. Really, I was sharpening my warrior skills so that I could use them to climb into the higher worlds.

No one died.

Those souls completed their mission of that particular incarnation.

Above all, I was not harmed. Because of those very days, I thrive now in the face of danger. Because of the tears I shed, I know that I am eternal, that all the power of the universe flows through me.

After this revelation, I step back into life with a strength I have never before known, true joy in doing my daily work, strength in meeting the challenges.

I have always adored the great, dark stories of *Wuthering Heights* and *Jane Eyre*. I knew Heathcliff's despair and Jane's fear of craziness in the attic. We all do—anyone who is driven to spirituality has walked the darkest path imaginable in order to arrive at the gates of freedom.

As I write this, I am free of that darkness. Now those experiences of my past are mostly neutral. They are but illusions that brought me to where I am today: living in a world of radiance lit by my Beloved inner self.

Soul for President

As leader I promise
no one will ever die
no one will ever go to Hell
no one will ever make a mistake
nor will anyone be punished…
only taught valuable lessons.

Under my guidance
all will enjoy…
lives of amazing adventure
days of boundless bliss
nights of quiet communion
a sense of Oneness with all creation
limitless love.

How can I make such extraordinary promises?
They are already true.

I invite you to view the video of this poem at www.lesleysking.com/2012/11/soul-for-president-2.

Where There's a Hill, There's a Way

Recently I got a new bicycle. It is shiny red and black with a little flame decal near the handlebars. Though I have been an avid cyclist since I was a child, for various reasons, I have not ridden in several years.

Now I am back in the saddle.

On my first day, I head into the vast network of trails near my house. Tingly happiness courses through me as I follow a dirt road that I often hike.

Since it's my first day, I intend to play it safe by staying on this road, but I see a single track veer to the left, and I take it. Suddenly my heart stirs and my palms grow moist as I head into the unknown.

I immediately call on my Master to accompany me on this adventure.

I am completely awake. My concentration zeroes in on the winding path before me that leads ever upward.

The track turns left and squeezes between two massive piñon trees and then climbs a small hill. I downshift to make it to the top.

Because I am awake, I negotiate each obstacle with ease. I upshift before an arroyo, or dry creek bed, and keep pedaling so I don't sink in the sand.

When I come to a steep descent, I brake fast with both the front and the back, keeping my bike in balance.

A snake crosses the path, brown diamonds on its back.

A rattler?

My throat constricts, but I see no rattle. It's only a bull snake. To avoid hitting it, I veer onto the grass.

A cool breeze blows across my neck, while the sun warms my cheeks.

A jackrabbit races alongside me, and though I appreciate the beauty as it bounds, I do not let it steal my concentration.

I climb and climb.

I yell, "whoop" over whoop-de-doos (little hills in a series), and I scream around banked curves.

Occasionally my mind darts away. It thinks of work or friendship or family. Under me, my bike wavers, it bumps on a rock, and I recognize I must hold my concentration or I will go down.

Everything depends on this moment.

I trust the Divine to take care of my finances, my relationships, my home, my whole life. All that matters is what is before my face.

It is enough for me to negotiate what is in this moment.
It is everything for me to be right here, right now.
I work, I play, I love on God's great single track.
I arrive at the summit. Piñon forest stretches below me, with sapphire mountains in the distance—all obstacles gone.
I breathe the radiant glee that I am.

Launch In

I wake in the dark at midnight, my mind with an imperative command: Launch my novel, *The Baby Pact*.

The thought is so unyielding and potent that I throw aside my covers to climb out of bed so I can head to my computer.

Yes, I will do a launch, and I will begin NOW.

As part of my indie authors' course, I learned how to team together with other writers so that on launch day thousands of people (ideally) learn about your book.

The sales drive your Amazon rating up, and, in one day, you become a best-selling author.

I have seen the concept work a number of times. Just yesterday, a colleague of mine succeeded with her launch. That fact sparks the ambition that now holds my attention.

But as I listen to the quiet surrounding my home, and a coyote yowling in the distance, something in this potential project rings false.

Really? I ask my mind. Am I to get up now and begin a launch?

Yes, most definitely, it says. You must!

Hmmm.

I call on the Beloved, and my mind relents just enough for a streak of light to shine through.

In fact I am adept at launching into the outer world. Many times in my life, rather than deal with the more subtle reality within—pain of lost loves, discomfort with a mate or job—I have launched to graduate school, to work in Asia, to travel around the globe. I have left jobs, homes, and relationships in order to create new ones.

All of that was perfect. No regrets.

But what if, this time, this singular now, I do something different?

What if I launch inward?

Rather than climb out of bed, I lie still. I breathe. I put on a spiritual CD and listen. My mind resists. It keeps thinking of all the tasks it will do in the launch, all the emailing and list making and copywriting. But I bring it back to the word of my Master.

Again and again.

The CD's message is about associating with love and thereby becoming it.

In the quiet of that directive, I settle. I feel my body and realize it is vibrating with fear, as though a hive of bees buzzes in my core.

I am afraid I will fail.

I am afraid I will run out of money.

I am afraid there is not enough love.

The ambition that has ruled my life has been mostly fear.

In this moment, I am turning that ambition toward my true self. And with that act, light dawns.

What if sustenance—survival—really does not have to take such sacrifice?

What if, instead, I make that sacrifice for my Beloved? What if I create love?

What if I really am sustained by love?

Suddenly I feel as though I have emerged through a dark layer of clouds into the luminous sunshine.

I soar in the freedom of that reality.

Life can be gentle and easy.

In each moment, I choose.

The CD ends and I drift off to sleep. In the morning I rise and open my blinds to a new matrix, a new day.

I will likely do a launch, but it can be a balanced activity, and it doesn't have to keep me up at night.

We are rockets with the power to launch into the heavens, to hurl ourselves to our sacred home. Any moment that I claim that power and direct it inward, I become the very love that I am.

God's Triple-Tiered Love Cake with Ecstasy Icing

*The wound is the place where
the Light enters you.*

—Rumi

Today is my mother and brother's birthday. For our little brunch party at my mother's house, I supply dessert: chocolate cake layered with mousse.

Though my mouth salivates at the sight of the delicacy, do I dare eat it?

At this point in my life, even a little dessert causes weeks of discord with my physical body and thus the rest of my life. This karma layer cake is likely the culmination of a lifetime (lifetimes?) of reliance on such food.

Years ago a boyfriend said to me, "There's no emotion at your ranch, there's just cake."

He was completely right. In my household as a child and well into adulthood, emotion was a force so powerful that it could not be entertained lest it take over. Rather than feel the pain of my yearning for God, I reached for food.

I baked sour-cream chocolate cake, chocolate cheesecake with cookie crust, chocolate cream pie layered with pecans, chocolate-chip walnut cookies, and much more. At our ranch house, we had a cart that I would wheel out after dinner to display all the delicacies. I ate while I baked, while I served, and while I did the dishes.

That matrix continued through my life. As an adult, I wrote about restaurants. Master chefs served me five-course meals that culminated in tiramisu, house-made coffee ice cream, or Grand Marnier chocolate mousse, to name only a few.

Only recently have I come to more peace with my emotional nature, so I no longer picture chocolate in my imagination during times of pain. Instead, I call on the Friend and sit and watch my emotions with compassion and patience.

This freedom has come as a gift from my devotion.

At our little party, I light the candles, carry out the cake, and initiate singing "Happy Birthday."

I'm grateful that my emotions can now work for me. When I yearn for love, instead of reaching for cake, I reach for God. And I let my emotions play across the image of my Master, and thus I fly into the higher worlds.

Today, while my family members savor the layers of chocolate, I eat a baked pear and enjoy what is truly important: my loved ones' company.

Someday I may be blessed with the ability to eat cake. For now I am blessed with the greatest of all confections: divine love.

Birth of a Dream

I hear the low groan of the UPS truck, followed by a thump on my porch. When I open the door, I find a box from my publisher, CreateSpace. I call on the Beloved and take a deep breath. Then I haul the box inside, grab a knife, and slash open the tape.

Inside I find twenty copies of my novel, *The Baby Pact*. I pull one out and hold it between my palms, feel its weight, marvel at the beauty of the cover, with a baby's face and a desertscape. My heart swells with exultation. It is perfect, a graceful reflection of an experience I had that I hope will inspire others.

When I was young, I always assumed I would have the whole pie. I worked as a journalist, played in the wilds of New Mexico's rivers and mountains where I kayaked, skied, biked, climbed, and ran, and I traveled the world. But I longed for the missing piece: a mate and child. The yearning felt like a chasm at the center of my being.

As I neared age forty, which felt like the cutoff date for this life experience, the desire intensified. This is the seed for *The Baby Pact*.

During this time, my best friend had twins, so I waded into that world. I listened to her complaints about sleepless nights and the pain of breastfeeding. At her home, I held her babies, smelled their milky scent, and helped change their diapers.

There were moments of beauty so rich I cried—the warmth of a baby against my chest, her pointy shoulder blades on my palm. And there were moments when I saw the immense challenge of parenthood. Most memorable was when the twins pooped their way through three diaper changes in a matter of minutes, while their screams pierced my eardrums.

The time I spent with my friend and her babies expanded my understanding. I vicariously tasted the duality of parenthood—its poignant beauty and its immense sacrifice. Throughout this time, I stayed close to the Infinite, asking for guidance.

One day, I realized that being a mother would not fill the void within me. Rather than a living child, I gave birth to this novel. More than a decade of nurturing went into it.

What drives good fiction is when a character has an unyielding desire for something. So my main character, Jamie O'Leary, heads into the procreative world with blind intensity.

Such extreme desire usually has roots in a past experience. Jamie's quest takes her back to her family ranch and a lost love.

The book tells a story that is familiar to us all—the painful path along which our passions lead us. We seek, we find. We become disappointed, lost, and bereft. From this, clarity is born. It happens again and again, until one day we arrive at our true self—that part that is pure love.

We stop searching.

We are found.

This is Jamie's story in *The Baby Pact*.

As I hold the book in my hands, gratitude fills me. I now know the true child I am to nurture: soul.

Unconditional Love

I am safe and loved
no matter what is happening
with my physical body,
with my house,
with my family and friendships,
with my job.
I am eternal.
I am love.

Bear the Love

Sometimes my cat, Arjuna, jumps up on my desk and saunters between my computer screen and me.

Sometimes when I cook, she meows and meows while tangling herself around my ankles.

Sometimes while I race to the door en route to a meeting or the grocery store, she leaps up and wraps her legs around my thigh.

Often during these pleas for love, I stop, take her in my lap, and run my palm over her back. With my fingertips, I massage the top of her head and under her chin. For moments she melts with my touch. She closes her eyes and purrs. She presses her ear into my palm and rolls over to expose her belly.

She accepts the love.

But suddenly her eyes widen. She lifts her head, leaps up, and scurries away.

I've come to accept this cat idiosyncrasy—kittyiosyncracy? And I see myself reflected.

The Divine waits ready to caress me. Any moment I ask, the love is there. And I do partake. I come into the stillness. My forehead, chest, belly, thighs, and toes relax. An easy smile curves across my lips, and my third eye shimmers. I ascend in wingless flight.

And just as suddenly, my mind leaps up and scurries away. It thinks about the conflict with my neighbor, a comment to write on Facebook, winter squash for lunch, or the evening news on television.

These diversions steal me from my Master. But they need never do so, even as I tend to them: I remain neutral with my contentious neighbor. I write loving posts on Facebook. I savor every bite of squash as a divine gift. And I hold my Beloved's hand while watching the play of duality on the TV news.

In every moment, I choose my attitude and where to put my attention.

My goal is to bear the love.

To enter it and never leave.

To be it.

Diamonds Aren't Forever but Love Is

Today I'm going out to sell diamonds. It is part of a whole process in which I'm giving away and selling things that no longer serve my life.

Besides that more lofty reason, I could use the cash.

The diamonds are gifts from a time when my family and I valued such things. Though I never wear them, I have over the years held onto them like a safety net.

I arrive in a notable jewelry shop just off the Santa Fe Plaza. The jeweler, a young woman with short blond hair and clear green eyes, pulls out her loupe and examines the first diamond—one of a pair of stud earrings.

My heart pounds as I await her assessment. Lately, I have held onto the idea that these diamonds might fund a few more months of my writing for The Inner Adventure. *The Baby Pact* is selling well, I'm coaching a few writers, and a bit of money comes in from managing my mother's home, but right now those are my only sources of income.

The jeweler clicks her tongue and nods and then picks up the second stud. As she examines it, she shakes her head.

I feel the tentacles of my desire and center on the Master.

The jeweler says one of the pair is faulty—worth next to nothing. The other, however, is a nice diamond. Disappointed, but not defeated, I hold out the third one that is a family heirloom. I have confidence in its worth.

As she examines the diamond set in a simple gold ring she smiles. "Yes, this is a quality diamond," she says. "But it is old."

I see that it doesn't hold the brilliance of the diamonds that surround me in this shop. They glitter with such intensity that the whole room radiates with luminous colors, like thousands of rainbows reflecting off each other.

The jeweler hands me the loupe and invites me to look. I view the gem up close—a stunning rock. In this moment, I realize diamonds are the highest valued item known. People give them as a precious gift to celebrate wedding engagements and anniversaries. Diamonds are the most treasured thing in the material world.

And yet…

While I gaze at the many prisms, the jeweler explains that this stone was hand cut. Today, through the precision of machine cutting, gemologists awaken much brighter sparkle, she says. Thus all the glitter surrounding me.

"We would not buy these diamonds," she explains kindly. Again my heart sinks. However, she does recommend an antiques dealer down the street.

When I ask her the value, she says maybe $200 to $400. What?

Honestly I had estimated thousands. And in its day, the heirloom may have been worth the equivalent of that. But even a diamond, the most prized of stones, the most durable and lasting gem, doesn't hold value.

I go to one antique dealer and another. Both offer what the first jeweler estimated.

I head to lunch with a friend. While we lounge on a cushy couch in her living room, she tells me that she has a check for $100,000 that she will deposit in the bank today. It is one of many from the business that she and her husband own, which is worth millions.

She tells me that when she holds the check, it feels heavy, full of weight. "When you have such money," she says, "you have to protect it, so you don't lose it, and so no one steals it."

I know that weight. I have felt it with these diamonds over the years, and with other possessions.

"It's the reliance," I say. "When we rely on such things, life becomes perilous."

In contrast, when I rely on the Beloved, it feels just the opposite. It's like a great opening into eternity. Rather than some bank account or some silly stone, I am relying on the Infinite, the very power that creates banks and jewels.

We laugh at the peril. It has no hold over us. We are immortal and eternal, with a power at our fingertips that outshines the most precious of stones.

As I leave her home, I suddenly have a vision of the jewelry shop's shimmering diamonds, shining their rays in a billion directions, with all the colors of the universe reflected.

I am that.

Maybe, now that I don't fear losing them, I will wear my diamonds, a reflection of my stunning inner radiance.

The "Hell Yes" Test

I sit across the table from Dave, who asked me out to tea. He talks of his work as an architect, and I talk of mine as a writer. We discuss our favorite pastimes, him riding horses, me hiking and biking.

"What's central to my life," I say, "is my spiritual path."

He nods and takes a bite of his muffin.

We finish our tea, hug, and say farewell.

The next day, he calls to tell me what a nice time he had. He wants to get together again. Sure, I say. Let's do that. But after I hang up, I stall like an engineless plane in midair.

Yes, he is nice, successful, and we've been acquaintances for years, so I know he's not an ax murderer. But I have to check to see if he passes the "Hell Yes" test.

The "Hell Yes" test—actually coined the "Hell Yeah" test by the brilliant entrepreneur Derek Sivers—suggests that when faced with an activity, if one doesn't say, "Hell yes, I want to do it!" then why bother?

When Dave calls again, I politely decline his invitation to go out because I am lukewarm about the idea. Sure, I can go and start up a new friendship, but why?

More and more I find that as I keep my attention on what engages me completely, which always includes the Master, the less I want to put my attention on the lukewarm things. That doesn't mean that I quit my current work or stop helping friends and relatives in need when those activities become challenging or dull.

It does mean that, as I keep directing my attention toward those things I'm most passionate about, day by day, all transforms into one big "Hell Yes!"

How to Travel Home

Take the Love Road.
It's best not to turn right or left.
But if you do, no problem.
While you travel the byway,
never forget the Love Road.
Eventually, you will merge back.

Stop for meals only at Love Diners
and sleep only in Love Motels.

When you know nothing but love
and have become love itself
unpack your bags
and live for eternity.

Alternate route:
Be love now.

I Am the Creator

Today I turned down the book contract with that photographer whom I met up with at the coffee shop. Even as I write this, I shake my head, incredulous. This might very well be an author's greatest sin.

But I had to.

The Master has shown me that the physical world is practice. It is the playground where I hone my skills that ultimately take me into the higher worlds, where love rather than force rules.

When I look back on my life, I see this powerful truth in action. Previously I wrote about the experience of when I taped onto my wall a photo of pyramidal peaks in China and within six months found myself there.

That experience marked the beginning of my conscious practice at being the creator. I imagined other lands: Bali, Thailand, Borneo, Nepal, Kenya, and Bolivia, and before long

I set foot in those places. Of course I bore all the challenges that come with travel: loneliness, discomfort, noise, frustration, and illness, but I also partook of spectacular beauty and adventure.

Now I take the same energy that went into those creations and direct it inward toward the True Creator. That is why I turned down the book contract.

As I ventured into the experience, I saw how much energy it was taking, to write the proposal, apply for grants because it paid little, and meet with my collaborator to discuss the complexities of the project. Above all, I wasn't passionate about the subject. I would have been writing about White Sands National Monument, a beautiful place, yes, but nothing compared to the beauty of the inner that I write about in my blog.

The project just didn't pass the "Hell Yes" test.

As well, the book would have required that I travel, stay in hotels, and eat diner food. Though a part of me can still enjoy a good road trip, right now my health doesn't tolerate such excursions. They make me ill and sap my energy and thus my spiritual connection.

Instead, I choose to direct that energy to staying home—not my material house, but my stationing in soul.

My decision to turn down the book contract is not an act of denial, but of love. I have written books, I have traveled, and through those acts I have come to know that the adventure, wealth, recognition, and love that I sought in the broad world can be had in any moment right within me.

Best of all, that love is free of deadlines, picky editors, delayed flights, road rage, and stomach aches.

It is a love that sees beauty in all of creation, a love that allows everyone and everything space to be themselves, a love that seeks nothing but to give itself away.

It is God.

So what happens when I direct that love inward?

I get to outflow here in this book, while I sip tea and wear bedroom slippers.

Most importantly, I get to write about what I love most: the Master.

I can only imagine the power of redirecting all that outward-bound energy to my true self.

But where will I get money, you ask?

That question is not for me to answer. I simply show up and be willing to channel this love in whatever way the Divine would have me.

Already I'm seeing my new creation take form. My subscriber list for The Inner Adventure is growing, and the reader reviews of my novel, *The Baby Pact*, are stellar.

But I don't have to worry over the details. In the same way the Beloved gave me a plane ticket to China some twenty-five years ago, that power will also give me exactly what I need today.

In fact, it already has.

Let the War Rage

Years ago, my father, who was a great fan of US history, told me that President Abraham Lincoln chose *not* to end the Civil War because he knew if the pressure were off, the amendment to the US Constitution abolishing slavery would not happen.

I never fully understood what my father meant until I saw the movie *Lincoln*. One doesn't have to see the movie to appreciate the beauty of this example. I can simply look to my own journey.

How often I wish for just a breath of peace, a moment when the war of life might calm. But it doesn't. My work, health, family, friendships, house—within these realms, battle always rages. These days the wars are more quiet than in years past, and yet they still persist.

Of course they originate within me; each skirmish illuminates yet another place where I'm holding to some idea of finding love and safety outside myself, rather than inside with the True Love.

In the movie, President Lincoln rides his horse through a battlefield strewn with bodies. His tall, lean figure bends with the weight of those deaths, which really are upon his shoulders.

In that image, I see the Master observing the carnage of my life. That Divine Power knows how the war hurts me. And yet if the pressure were to abate even for a moment, if a peace were declared, all my incentive to reach higher within myself, to stretch beyond my limited beliefs—to fly—would die.

And thus would perish my spiritual journey.

I am here to ratify the amendment to my own constitution that abolishes my slavery. Such an act ends my reliance on the dual worlds, worlds that distinguish between black and white, rather than admitting to the great Oneness that we all are.

And so, each day I wake, do my spiritual practice, and enter the battlefield with the Beloved at my side. I am a great soldier of love, fighting in every moment for my freedom.

And with each moment that I stay in the divine now, I win.

Like a star in the sky, I sit high above all duality, all condition.

It is no tragedy that President Lincoln left this plane just two months after his great victory of abolishing slavery. His mission was complete, just as one day my imprisonment in the lower worlds will be.

Merged back into God's limitless love, I will reside in complete peace.

Until then, let the war rage.

Game On

With a prompt from my publisher, I open a document and read the first unfavorable review for my novel, *The Baby Pact*. It is inevitable. I have received a number of positive ones, so I know a negative one must join the chorus. After all, that is the dual way of the lower worlds.

What surprises me is how much it hurts. As I read, I hold the Beloved's hand, but still, my heart sinks into my stomach and my arms and legs weaken. I tremble with a cold sweat.

All because I have relied on this review.

I paid for it with the hope of using it to further promote the novel. Suddenly, the folly of my reliance unveils.

Again and again at this point in my journey, I'm shown that I am to rely on nothing but the Infinite One to sustain me.

In the past I have been like an athlete in search of sponsorship. Elite swimmers, cyclists, and runners seek powerful brands such as Nike, Gatorade, and Rolex to sustain them, allowing them to focus completely on their sport. I too have found entities to subsidize me.

Frommer's travel guides, *New Mexico Magazine*, and a handful of other publications have paid me over the past few decades. I outgrew those sponsorships to the great relief of my subtler being.

And now, here I sit, sponsorless.

I had one little hope of a patron—this review. I hoped to use it as proof of the quality of my novel so that more readers would buy *The Baby Pact*.

Ironically, the reviewer expected the very things that my old sponsors did. He wanted more backstory, more of the characters' pasts. Principally, he wanted the characters to act in a more moral way.

In a similar way, the mind always wants me to operate from the dead imagery of the past, and to act from a place of right versus wrong, rather than truth.

Please understand that I'm all for improving my writing, but I sense this is about something deeper.

When I see how this experience is stealing my attention, satisfaction seeps in because I know I am unwinding karma.

I say "game on," and call on the Master.

Within a few hours of releasing this again and again, the wretched mental fog begins to lift. My limbs steady, my breath slows.

I recall that some of the most poignant and happy moments of my life were when an entity agreed to sponsor me: when Frommer's wrote to say they wanted to hire me; when *New Mexico Magazine* offered me a monthly column. In those moments, I radiated with pride over my accomplishments. Most importantly, I felt safe and loved.

It was like having a supportive father, a protector, a guide. However, with the agreement, the sponsor directed where I went and what I wrote—and what I didn't write. Under that care I was sponsored, but I was not free. I could write my truth only as it served the patron's interests.

So now, with the mental fog blown away, the True Sponsor comes into view. My body grows weightless with a sensation of safety and love, a feeling that far surpasses those material sponsorships.

I am so light, I float.

It's a new sensation. Worldly sponsorships always come with a stomach flutter and sweaty palms, a deep knowing that in the end I will give more than I receive.

When I rely on the divine sponsorship, the mind is still. My whole being settles into a glimmering wonder. The truth pours through, directing me where it wants me to go.

It does not push me to harm my body. It does not squelch my expression. In contrast, it expands, showing me that I am as broad as the entire universe. I am the stars and the distant galaxies. I am the essence that infuses all life.

I am love.

Scrooge Buys a Tree

Last year, just a few days after I bought a Christmas tree for my mother, it died. Its needles dried to a frank crispness; its color turned a dull sage. It shed itself onto the carpet and transformed into Charlie Brown's original tree.

All because I had a Scrooge attitude.

When I set out on my annual quest to buy the tree, my goal, I'm embarrassed to say, was to get it over with. I had better things to do. So I entered the Christmas tree yard, stepped toward the smaller trees and quickly chose one—it was fine.

This took very little time. However, when I erected the tree, problems began. I could not get it to stand straight and steady. And once it stood in my mother's living room, its fatal flaw emerged: at its center, a big branchless gap. I shrugged, kissed my mother good-bye, and headed home.

When I returned a few days later, it had died.

I blamed the tree seller—he likely didn't cut the base to allow the water in. But inside myself, I sensed a deeper cause at work.

So today I set out with a new matrix. It is a profound lesson I have learned over many years, but grasp yet more fully now: I perform every act in service to the Master.

That is now my joy, my energy, my life.

When I step into the Christmas tree lot, a smile fills my being. I smell the tangy scent of pine and feel the poignancy of this place.

The men and women who work here struggle with substance abuse. They live for a time at Delancey Street, a retreat in northern New Mexico, where they trade their addiction for a new life. These are people with nothing left to lose. I appreciate their humility because I too have been brought to my knees.

I walk the rows of trees, confer with a couple also looking for a six-footer. A kid with a shaggy head of sandy-colored hair helps me find a narrow tree to fit by my mother's piano. He is quiet and focused as he chainsaws the base and straps the tree to my car.

When I arrive at my mother's, I wonder how I will carry the long, bristly bundle inside, and I doubt my ability to erect it. But I call on the Omnipotence, and within moments I'm dragging it to the door. Like a sled, it glides easily on a blanket of snow. I pull the tree inside and recognize the most challenging part is upon me. Again I ask for help, and without even thinking, I put the stand on while the tree rests on its side. I tighten the screws with ease.

I take hold of the top and spring it into position. It stands straight, tall, and full. It is a proud and flawless tree.

My mother wheels in on her walker and looks it up and down. Tears well in her eyes. "It's the most beautiful tree I've ever seen," she says. And I agree, knowing I did nothing but show up willing to flow the Divine Current into this day.

All else was graced.

The life of service to the Beloved is a life of ease. I have nothing to get and only to give. I am an empty vessel channeling a limitless power. When I am willing to act in its name, that power provides all that I need. I don't worry about sustenance, energy, or money. All flow into my life when I am willing to flow them into the divine creation.

In service, I am free.

Waltz with the Master

With a phone to my ear, I pace from my kitchen to my living room and back. My palms sweat. My throat constricts, and my stomach churns. Occasionally a voice within says, "You're failing. This is terrible." But I ignore it, call on the Master and keep talking.

No, I'm not breaking up with a boyfriend, nor am I trying to convince the IRS that my deductions are honest.

I am being the creator.

This is really an inner movement in which I decide that I'm not going to sit on my duff and wait to be spiritual. Instead I take the Beloved's hand and launch into my Godliness.

Then I actuate the Divinity by launching in my outer life.

So I was guided to create a writing course. Rather than advertise it and wait for clients to pay, I simply did it. I planned the course and told my friends on my blog and on social media. Now I'm delivering it for free over the phone.

That's what my sweaty palmed call is about.

This extroverted experience isn't easy for me. I tend to have stage fright, and the virtual auditorium of a phone line only slightly eases the fear. For days before the course, my appetite deadened and my sleep felt as if I was a chicken on a rotisserie, turning and turning.

So now, when I hang up the line, I'm pleased. Some forty people tuned in. I created something with passion and put it out to the cosmos.

I head to my computer to see who has signed up—and paid—for the extended course I offered.

My heart sinks when I see that no one has.

I take a walk, return, and check again. My arms hang limply from their sockets, and my heart feels as though it's pressing up into my throat. I put so much effort into the free call and into planning my offering. But no one is signing up.

I have no choice but to surrender this. I give it to the Infinite One, eat dinner, and go to bed.

When I awaken, I do my spiritual exercise, and the weight eases. I see that it doesn't matter whether or not anyone signs up. What matters is my willingness to act in order to find out what will happen. I did my best to listen to divine guidance and to walk through the fear. In that light, my course was a complete success.

I also see that all love and wealth are within me. I am completely supported by the Sustainer.

As I cook breakfast, a quiet voice in me says, "I'll teach that course. It will be fun, instructive for me, and a great opportunity to channel divine love to the world." I don't know to whom I will teach, but that doesn't matter. Rather than a need or desire, this is a quiet knowing.

I open my email box, and there they are, my first clients, along with a few emails indicating more to come.

This is the dance of surrender and acting to find out.

When I was an adolescent, I learned to waltz, and I still enjoy it. My partner and I take long, gliding steps to the count of three. I yield to the pressure of his palm on my hip and shoulder, but I must manifest my own part. So I hold my frame and step to the beat. Together we float around the floor, our beings rising and falling as though on swelling waves. We disappear into the movement that is pure love.

This dance with the Master is how I come to be my true divine self.

The Beloved's Playlist

I awaken with a quiet lethargy. It tugs at me like a lead weight pulling me deep into the ocean. But I rise from my bed, do my spiritual practice, and head into the world.

I drive to the grocery store, and on my way, the weight bears down again. After a week of restless sleep and some health problems, I'm tired. For days I've been trying to find the courage to take the next step in my new work. In the upcoming weeks, I will begin teaching two sections of my writing course. I have technology to learn and new souls to meet.

However, today I don't want to participate in my life, much less be the master of it.

As I drive, I recognize this negative trap for what it is: a trick of the mind to keep me down. I call on the Friend. Immediately I get the nudge to turn on the radio. From it comes a song I've never heard by the New York City indie band Fun. The song urges me to "Carry on," no matter what, to let my past be the sound of my "feet upon the ground."

I park the car and say, "Yes, I can carry on!"

I grab my bags and water jugs and step into the store.

In the produce section, I pick up blueberries, spinach, jicama, and asparagus. Then I make my way to the bulk-food area.

While I select Turkish figs, the weight comes again. I am en route for a day of service to my mother, yet I'm having trouble even serving myself. Again I call on the Beloved, and suddenly over the Whole Foods speaker comes Bill Withers singing "Lean on Me."

He sings about how we all have pain and sorrow, but it's just this moment, and there will be a brighter tomorrow. The song reminds me that when I'm not feeling strong, I can lean on the Omnipotent One within. "I'll help you carry on," Withers croons.

Tears well in my eyes and drip onto my figs. I wipe my face on my sleeve, take a deep breath, and head to the meat counter.

The song provides solace, so I can give a genuine smile and thanks to the butcher who wraps my chicken. And I continue to hear the melody as I fill my water bottles and check out at the register.

While I drive to my mother's house, I realize I can meet today's challenge. I can make breakfast, feed and walk the dog, and do the accounting.

I can give love.

And suddenly over the radio comes boy band One Direction singing "What Makes You Beautiful." They sing of how they can see our beauty, the way we light up a room, but how we can't see our own. "That's what makes you beautiful."

Corny, definitely, but I'm reminded that I am beautiful inside, where it counts. I turn off the radio and listen to the silence while I make my way up a hill and park in front of my mother's house.

In the quiet, the true Sound rushes in, filling me with love. It's like floating on a cloud high above all. Goose bumps cover my skin, and a smile stretches across my face.

As I walk up the path to the house, my recent favorite song comes into my head: "Ho Hey" by the Lumineers. In the song I hear that I belong to my Beloved, and the Beloved belongs to me. When I cherish this true self, all the energy and power I need manifest.

I open the door, happily singing:
"I belong with you
You belong with me…
Ho hey, Ho hey."

The Great Conductor provides the song until I know the tune and can sing it to the world.

My day of service?
A total lovefest.

The Divine Court

While I stand in the center of my sunny living room, I open an envelope and unfold a letter. Immediately, I see the date—just two weeks away. I call on the Master but still feel the shift inside me. It's a darkness that spreads like black ink in water, weakening my arms so the paper trembles between my fingers. I make my way to the couch and sit down.

The letter from the Santa Fe Magistrate Court invites my neighbors and me to stand before a judge to argue our case against Dee, the woman on our community well who refuses to pay her bills.

It is simple, so why does it fill me with this dark dread?

Karma—that's why.

This situation mirrors my childhood. The neighbor, a woman who works on Wall Street, holds a similar bully vibration to my older sister. For the twenty-six years of her life, my sister and her rage held those around her hostage.

But it's not only her. Because I try to be so "nice," I have manifested a long line of bullies in my life, from students when I was a child, to coworkers, friends, and mates as an adult.

That bully vibration so intimidates me that I lose myself, and so I lose my "home."

This little letter, this court hearing, holds that threat. My mind, in its habitual way, thinks the outcome could mean the loss of my material home.

The woman, Dee, has promised to take everything from us. She threatened to sue us for all we have, offering as example a Canadian man she sued, winning his house and all his assets.

As well manager, I am to stand up to her.

I want to take a trip, drink red wine, find a man to deal with this—anything but stand before that judge.

Instead, I go to my computer and send out an email to my neighbors and our engineer witness. From my cabinet, I pull out the files of evidence I have gathered.

Over the next few days, my neighbors agree to attend, but the witness informs me that he will be traveling in Turkey. He is supposed to attest to the fact that I read the well meters properly, which is Dee's biggest contention.

She also complains of poor water pressure and insists that one well member does not belong on the well. Her list of reasons for not paying continually grows.

I have done my best to answer each contention, with evidence to back up our side. But is it enough? As I shuffle through the papers, the black dread creeps in again. I know that she has a ruthless attorney, whom I will have to face. Meanwhile, our attorney doesn't try cases in this court, so we are without a lawyer. I try to enlist another one to help, but he never gets back to me.

My mind wants to stay in the fight. It wants to go over all the reasons Dee is wrong and we're right. It also wants to enumerate my own mistakes over the years—most notably a few math errors that have become huge in my head.

Instead, I rivet my attention on the Omniscient One and on what's before me right here, right now.

Over the next few days, whenever I think of the hearing, my limbs again weaken. But one day, during my spiritual practice, I see that I want to rely on the witness and attorney, when really they are not the key to this.

All I really need in that courtroom is True Judge.

Suddenly, the weakness transmutes into strength, as I see that it doesn't matter whether we win or lose. All that matters is that I keep the Beloved close and tell the truth.

The morning of the hearing, I awaken from a deep sleep. Strength courses through my limbs. During my spiritual practice, I realize that I have already won, no matter what the judge determines.

This woman represents my material mind. She races among three homes scattered about the United States, her attention hostage to prestige and money. In degree, she represents the old me.

But the Master has graced me with new ideals: love, kindness, and balance. These now rule my life.

Just two days ago, the new attorney called to say he would present our case, and our witness informed us that he had changed his travel plans.

Accompanied by my mother, a posse of neighbors, the attorney, and witness, I step into the courtroom and sit at the plaintiff's table. The sterile room has maroon carpet, rows of seats in back, and a faux-wood judge's bench and witness stand in front. The scent of ammonia permeates the air.

We assumed Dee would be armed with her attorney, but she sits alone at the defendant's table, which is cluttered with paper.

When the judge enters, we all rise.

Our attorney presents our case, noting simply that the defendant does not pay her bills.

When Dee stands to present her case, I note how small she appears, with bleached hair and a frantic step. Her lips peel, her shoulders slump. She contends that there are many complexities to the case, most notably that we read her meter wrong.

Soon I am on the witness stand explaining our side. When Dee questions me, she asks about the mistakes I have made. My pulse quickens, but I steady myself. I call on the Master, remembering that I corrected each as soon as I noted the error. The issue evaporates.

When our attorney questions Dee, she evades answering and complicates the simplest issues. She fidgets in the witness box, bites her lips, and bats at her hair. Finally, the judge, exasperated, threatens her with 180 days in jail for contempt of court if she doesn't answer directly.

Our engineer witness attests to my correct meter readings. But when Dee cross-examines him, he leans toward her, as though mesmerized by her blue eyes and blond hair. She flirts with him, offering a coy smile. Suddenly his answers become confused, his words stuttery.

So once the closing arguments are complete, I wonder whether we have won or lost. Throughout five hours, I have kept the Beloved close, but still my body shivers with tension.

The judge sits forward in her chair and clears her throat. "It appears to me, based on your evidence," she says to Dee, "that you created all of these problems yourself, and you want to blame others."

In the judge's words, I can hear the resonant truth of that statement. The material mind, with its desires and attachments to the security of *things,* creates all its own problems.

"For that reason," continues the judge, "I rule in favor of the plaintiff." She orders Dee to pay the well charges and all attorney fees.

I sit back in my chair, the knots in my shoulders releasing. My neighbor, an old Hispanic man with diabetes-blue skin who has trouble hearing, taps me on the shoulder and asks what happened.

I smile at him and say, "We won."

Road to Freedom

Let's take the Mother Road,
tasting en route
the sparking-fat diners
the creaky court motels,
where we'll lay waste
to the flesh,
and carve our initials
in the illusion of love,
knowing the real thing
waits within
ignited by our Friend,
who's driving us home.

Make the Mind Your Friend

Today, for the first time, my mother's dog and my cat will meet. The prospect of this makes my shoulders clench and my heart pound. I want them to be friends, so that we can spend time together as a family.

Even more importantly, if my cat, Arjuna, could spend the days I care for my mother with me, I wouldn't return home in the evenings to a lonely pal who wants to play, when all I want is sleep.

But these two souls have polar energy: Mischief lives up to his name as a hyper Yorkie, who, like a dervish, spins around the house, over furniture, and under beds. He often barks and whines, but with his glistening, dark eyes and tiny smile, he wins hearts.

Meanwhile, Arjuna eschews chaos and, like Buddha, exudes calmness. She can be ruthless when her boundaries are threatened.

For weeks we have worked toward this moment. A handful of times I left Arjuna at my mother's while I took Mischief for a walk. This exposed them to each other's scents without yet meeting.

Until today, when I call on the Master and bring them together.

They first see each other through a window, the dog outside, Arjuna inside. Mischief leaps toward the glass, and Arjuna bolts. I lovingly catch her, so she must stay and see him—give him a chance—and she does. She takes two steps toward him, then scurries away.

Next I place her on the kitchen counter and invite Mischief in. While I cook potatoes and eggs for breakfast, the animals eye each other. When Mischief leaps upward at her, Arjuna crouches, hisses, and bears her fangs.

Mischief backs off and heads to the living room, while Arjuna seizes the opportunity to leap from the counter and run. I turn off the stove and follow.

They stand face-to-face in the hallway.

Uncertain what to do, I hover above them. Suddenly, Mischief lunges forward. Arjuna stretches out her front leg, bears her claws, and takes a grand swipe at his nose, missing by inches. Then she wheels around and runs.

Mischief chases. They tear around the living room, under the coffee table and in front of an antique chest.

This has been my fear—that the meeting of these two animals whom I cherish would end in war or, even worse, death.

They stop by the couch. Two feet apart, they're ready to fight. I kneel between them and speak in a low voice. "It's okay. You're safe."

I call on the True Mediator.

With my left hand, I pet Mischief from ears to tail, his fur bristly under my palm. With my right hand, I pet Arjuna, her fur soft as mink. The intensity settles, as though we are kneeling in a cloud of love. Around us the air smells rich and salty from my favorite comfort foods. My own heart settles.

I'm reminded of a line from the poem by the nineteenth-century saint Soami Ji Maharaj titled "Make the Mind Your Friend": "Let us place ourselves at His feet, you and me. Through that satsang we will gain something."

In this moment, we all bask in the love of the Divine Current.

This experience reflects my life these days. When a challenge arises, my first impulse is to flee or fight. But instead I sit at the feet of the Master. That loving force massages my neck and down my spine. It soothes until my mind settles and becomes friendly.

Thus a new reality emerges: love.

In this alternative place, there are no mistakes and no differences, only One great whole, whose song we dance to throughout eternity.

I stop petting these sweet souls, and they tentatively stand. Arjuna turns and slinks away, finding a hiding place near an overstuffed chair. Meanwhile, Mischief scurries off in search of my mother.

No doubt there will be more such meetings in their lives and my own. During each, I will bring in the divine love to soothe and calm until I fully know that I am It.

The Lover's Breath

How could I ever forget
the weight of my basalt self nestled against the earth?

How could I forget
the arc of my great whale body as it skims the ocean floor?

How could I forget
the whoosh of my feathery wings while they flap in flight?

Most of all,
how could I forget
the Lover's breath on my neck as I sleep?

All In For Love

All exists here, now
The rock
Whale
Dove
Lover
Love.

Born into each, a flicker of memory,
then
the avalanche
the razor teeth
ripped flesh
catapult from the sky
bruised heart
dim all
until I sleep in the dark
of bone and skin of a new body.

This is true
I think as I dive deeper and deeper
into the dream of what I am not.

It is not God who erases the truth,
but me.

The flame always burns.
It is I who
leave its illuminating glow.

Lesley S. King

Of course I forget.
Just as any moment I can again remember
the all of creation that
I am.

Sustained by Love

My mother and I sit in cushy chairs across a broad desk from a psychiatrist. He is a kind man with ruddy cheeks and curly gray hair. A collection of blown-glass art pieces adorns his desk and shelves.

"I don't want to pay her," my mother says.

I call on the Sustainer of all.

I'm surprised that this is to be our topic today, since I thought that months ago we had settled this issue of her paying me to run her household. But fury again sparks in her eyes, and again my heart aches.

A month ago I got an emergency call from her caregiver who arrived to find my mother passed out on the hall floor. I rushed over, and together the caregiver and I woke her and got her back into bed. A look at her medications showed she'd taken half a bottle of a new prescription of sleeping pills.

We debated whether or not to take her to the hospital, and in retrospect we should have. For two days we stayed on twenty-four-hour watch, helping her to and from the bathroom and attempting to get her to eat. It was grueling.

Throughout, we were in contact with her doctor. Once my mother had recovered, the doctor insisted that she come under the care of a psychiatrist who could more closely monitor her depression and mental-related medications. The doc gave me a list of geriatric specialists, and this man was the only one who could see her soon.

He was perfect for her.

What most surprised us both was that often I would sit in on the sessions. Initially, I stayed to help with clarifying what was going on with her, but soon the meetings transformed into helping both of us work through issues like this one that has arisen today.

"So why don't you want to pay her?" the doctor asks my mother.

"I've always thought we were a team," she says.

She turns toward me, and I can see the hurt in her eyes, as they pinch at the corners. I sense it's caused by a break in the trust that she has relied on between us. It's true, we have been a team, through our travels and through her cancer and my allergies. I have supported her with my physical strength, and she has at times helped me out financially. We have both helped each other through emotional trials too—her estrangement from my brother, my challenges with mates.

We talk more, about how she intends to leave me her house, about how caring for her cuts into my work time, making it hard for me to make a living. And then for a few moments, we sit quietly, a cool breeze blowing in through the window. The room is comfortably shadowed because the doctor leaves the lights off.

He says to me, "What makes you think you have to be paid? What if you trusted that you would be okay?"

I close my eyes and ask for the Master's viewpoint. A sense of calm settles my heart, and I suddenly see my family, how it was growing up. There was always a sense that we had to work for our keep. Ours was never a family that celebrated children for the wonder that they are, where the kids had a sense that they existed simply because their parents loved them.

The religion of our family was not Christianity or Judaism, but instead capitalism. We all bowed to the mighty dollar. I started earning money as a little girl. For a quarter an hour, I raked and pulled weeds around the house, and when I was thirteen, I began punching a time clock for the labor I did on our family ranch. This work ethic has served me well in my life, but maybe now it's outdated.

Within, the Sustainer asks, "What if you don't have to be paid? What if you leave your sustenance to me?" A rush of appreciation fills me as I realize that my Beloved is the true and loving parent. I exist because of Its love for me, and for no other reason. I don't earn my existence or struggle for survival. Instead I rest in the palms of love. A sense of freedom like a clear, cool waterfall washes over me.

I turn to my mother and say, "You're right, you don't need to pay me." And I truly mean it. My rapture for the Beloved spills out to fill the whole room, and the forgiveness between us shines luminous.

As I help my mother to the car, the blue sky and the bare winter trees shimmer with promise. My true Father provides all I need, always and forever, while I convey love into the world. I can serve my mother and leave the rest to God.

Forgive Your Vanity

*Forgiveness is the fragrance the violet
sheds on the heel that crushed it.*

—Mark Twain

I awaken from my first full night of sleep in weeks. Lemony sun shines in the window, and when I stand, I feel a hint of the life force that faded during my two-week illness. In my spiritual practice, my body fills with luminosity, a lightness of being that is pure freedom.

But afterward, when I look in the mirror, I see the toll of these weeks. Blue shadows hang below my eyes, and a mustard tint masks my skin.

Normally I would shrug this off, but today it matters. In just a few hours, I am to sit in front of a video camera to give a testimonial for my dentist.

I call on the Beautiful One and remember that I am soul.

It is no big deal, I tell myself as I apply powder to my cheeks. I smooth away the blotchy patches. I conceal the shadows under my eyes. With a mascara wand, I take extra strokes, as I do with my lipstick. I even dig through the back of my closet to find a curling iron to add life to my limp hair.

I'm ready.

The videographer, who is one of my closest friends, encourages me through the session. "You look fabulous!" she says. I happily voice praise of my dentist and friend of twenty years, Dr. Richard Parker. It's a wrap. The videographer packs up her camera and heads out, while I go on with my day.

The next afternoon I receive a link to a rough cut of the video. When my testimonial comes on, I gasp. I look like a faded waif, pale, with too much lipstick and eye makeup. The lighting is so bright it melds me into the yellow wall behind. I take a breath and recognize my vanity.

It's fine, I tell myself. No problem. I send a congratulations email to the videographer.

But over the next few hours, my mind will not let it go. It's as though Norma Desmond from *Sunset Boulevard* has occupied my insides and keeps calling for a new close-up.

I take a walk and with each step call on the Master. I talk to my vanity in an attempt to get it to stand down. I recognize that I am more than this physical body, and yet I can't let the issue go. To compound it, I have heard my friend discuss her challenges with shooting baby boomers over the years, who often scorn their video appearance. I don't want to be like them.

It's the lighting, that's the problem, I determine. When I arrive home, I send an email to the videographer saying the light was too bright—it blazed out the midtones. We have to reshoot.

I receive an immediate reply. She is pleased with the outcome—no reshoot necessary. Her message carries the same cutting vibe as did the one I sent. Of course, we always get back what we give.

I'm infuriated with her reply. "Can't she see?" I ask my cat.

I pace my kitchen. By now night has settled in. I suspect my sleep is in jeopardy, and with it my fragile remission from my recent health challenge. Worse yet, my dear friend is now upset with me, and I with her.

My mother calls and, after hearing my dilemma, suggests an impasse. I follow her counsel. With what little humility I can muster, I email my friend. I tell her I love her, admit that I'm sorting through this, and ask her to simply hold until I'm clear.

I sleep a few hours and awaken, my limbs restless. So I rise at midnight and ask the Beloved to guide me. With that loving presence at my side, I sweep the floor, prune the geraniums, and clean a linen closet. While I do this, shards of illusion present themselves. I see how much I have relied on my appearance in order to secure love, from my family, in relationships, and in my work as a journalist.

Finally truth unveils: I recognize that the love is within me, not something that comes from without. I return to bed to sleep a few more hours.

I awaken with an odd peace. During my spiritual practice, more truth ignites. Maybe it's okay that I care how I look in the video. Maybe it's fine that I'm vain. My physical appearance, my vanity, these are only small spokes on the great wheel of who I am. I can accept and love those parts.

I go to my computer and tentatively open an email from my friend the videographer.

"Lesley," she writes. "Let's do a reshoot, whenever you're feeling better. I am in no hurry."

My heart settles.

The reshoot will come, and likely I won't be thrilled with my fifty-something appearance. But maybe I'll look a little healthier. Most importantly, I will know that I am not this physical body, nor am I this vanity. Instead I am the very life force itself, on a great journey through eternity.

I am pure beauty in spirit.

I am soul.

Eternal love.

Own Your Power

Most every day I take a walk through the piñon-juniper forest surrounding my house. On today's journey, I melt into the quiet. Finches chirp and flit among the treetops, puffy clouds skate across the sky, and the azure Sandia Mountains stand tall in the distance.

As I pass some horse stables, where the air smells beer-like from the manure, a dog races over a hill straight toward me. He is midsized with a blue-merle coat. Head down, hackles raised, tail flagging, he means business. My heartbeat accelerates, and my palms become damp. Immediately I call on the Beloved and hold my hand up in front of me like a traffic cop signaling "stop." The dog pauses, paces sideways, and growls.

Through the years of my spiritual path, I have learned to use my mantra as a means to ward off attacks, whether from animals or people. In dreams, a simple uttering of the Master's name dismantles all adversity. Similarly, in my waking life, if a colleague, family member, or neighbor comes at me with anger and I chant my mantra, the situation diffuses. Either love comes in and calms all, or the person suddenly hangs up the phone or leaves.

I am protected.

Today, however, the dog stays. I keep my hand up while I silently chant. He circles me, bears his fangs. He backs off, lunges at me. I yell for an owner to call him away, but no one answers. I walk backward, my front always toward him. He circles again, and again I chant my mantra.

For an instant I consider that he actually might bite me. The image crosses my screen—torn flesh, blood, pain. A tremor of fear runs through my body.

I have to take more extreme measures, I realize. Without even making a decision, I suddenly envision myself as the Master. My posture straightens so that I feel over six feet tall. My being settles into a state of loving strength.

Within seconds, the dog's tail lowers. The fury in his eyes softens. He turns and slinks away, his back curved in submission.

I'm astonished as I continue to walk, glancing back every few steps. His eyes track me, but now he stays lower to the ground, making his way over the hill from where he came.

It occurs to me that these days my lessons are like this. Where once it was enough to simply call for help, now I am asked to be the help, to own my true power, to wear it, walk within it, live it.

When I return home, I recognize that for much of the day I have been under attack, not from a dog, but from myself. Since my recent health challenge, I have chosen to relax more, to rely on the Beloved. But this day, my mind has its own agenda. It wants me at my computer, writing, editing, and corresponding. Rather than stand up to this force, I've avoided it, hoping the pushy, biting vibration would leave.

Of course the dog manifested as that vibration in physical form.

Once I recognize its more subtle presence within, I call on the Omnipotent One and chant my mantra. The dark force growls just as loudly as did the dog. It does not want to leave. In its presence, my heart races. I remain steadfast, though, before it while owning my True Strength.

Suddenly, it disappears over some inner hill.

I move into a state of pure love. I know that all comes from the Divine Power, not from my little efforts on the material plane.

I am the power of all creation. Any time I own it, I am it.

The Sky of Love

The mind is a book,
a maze of sentences
set in a state of permanence
from which it cannot escape itself.

The Beloved is an azure sky
with cauliflower clouds
anvil thunderheads, swirling tornados
raindrops, hail, sleet
blazing sun—
a rainbow.

All In For Love

This true Love is still
fluid, adaptable—
ready
with the
perfect
action
in the
now.

The Soul Emergency

It's Saturday night, and just as I settle under the bed covers, the phone rings. I pick up and hear the voice of my mother's caregiver. "She has a nosebleed that's not stopping."

I call on the Master.

My mom comes on the line. "I'm pressing the button," she says, meaning her Life Line, a signal that sends nearly a dozen people into immediate action. Within fifteen minutes, five emergency responders stand in her bedroom, an ambulance and fire engine rumbling in the driveway.

Her private nurse receives notice and heads there too. Meanwhile, at my house, I pull on leggings and a sweatshirt, say good-bye to my cat, and head to the hospital, sensing that this may be a long night.

The ER doc stops the bleeding, and just after midnight, I settle Mom back in bed at her home. But in the coming days, the sense of emergency increases. My mother already breathes oxygen from a machine twenty-four hours a day, yet in the coming days, she can't seem to get enough.

On Tuesday, after a few restless nights of sleep, I struggle to keep pace with the directions from her nurse and caregiver. All want to fix this problem. They want her calm, breathing, alive. And she, of course, wants that more than anyone, so with her will and fear, she pushes, she wants. She is like a drowning victim gasping for breath.

And yet…her oxygen levels are okay.

We have set an appointment to see a pulmonary specialist on Thursday, and I hope this will bring some understanding.

At my home, I'm lying on the couch trying to gather back some energy when the nurse calls. Tired, I barely grasp the details: she has set up an appointment for a medical evaluation, and she wants me there at 3:00 p.m. I listen, say okay, and hang up.

Suddenly, a surge of anger rushes through me. It's a fiery fury that manifests in a scream. I don't know what it is about, but I cannot ignore it. I want to go outward with it, yell at the nurse. Tell her I'm exhausted, I'm not going. After years of caring for my mother, I fear I can no longer prop her up, be her strength. Instead of yelling at anyone, I call on the Master.

I take out a spiritual contemplation note and read it, directing my attention off my anger and onto the loving message on the printed page. My mind wants to stay in the fury, but slowly it submits to the love. I finish the reading in a state of peace.

I go to the kitchen to make lunch. As I cut a beet, a lightning bolt of truth strikes.

"There is no emergency," the Omniscience whispers. "It is all perfect. Your mother is experiencing the expiration of her physical body. It is a beautiful piece of the whole of life, completely natural, wonderfully loving, all in sync with the divine plan."

I see how the nurse simply doesn't know of my mother's eternity, and so I forgive her pushing. And my mother doesn't know, so I forgive her neediness.

She is a soul with so much life yet to experience. Soon she will leave her physical body, which is bed-bound, and enter into a new incarnation, where she can enjoy the adventures that still ignite her imagination.

As I eat my lunch, I feel my own life force return. I can easily be there for her during the medical evaluation and during this whole transition. In the next few days, I keep the Beloved close as I do my best to follow the guidance in each moment.

I can love her and let her go.

I see how this sense of emergency around mortality reflects my own mind's panic, as I let go yet more of my attachment to the material world. My passion for possessions, prestige, and satiating my body's hungers, though still present, dwindles daily as I come to more deeply desire the Master. As I let go, mind mobilizes untold emergency responders within me. It wants to run away to a tropical beach, find another soul to lean on, drink red wine, and eat chocolate.

Meanwhile, soul only desires to bathe in the soothing Current of divine love.

When systems fail, sometimes we need to push the button and bring in the emergency teams, but there is only one true emergency, one imperative in every now: to leap into the Beloved's arms.

Now, in the darkness of early dawn, I sit by my mother's hospital bed. Forty-eight hours ago, at the urging of her doctor, I brought her to the ER, where the medical team informed me she would soon depart. Since then, my siblings and I have held an around-the-clock, tag-team vigil, as my mother lay unconscious.

I hold my iPhone, which plays soothing music. My mother looks beautiful lying here, her eyebrows dark on a face that is exquisitely pale. I do not hold her hand because a hospice friend told me it is best not to enliven the limbs from which she has already withdrawn her energy. But I do watch her breath, which is light, barely moving the covers on her chest.

I close my eyes and inside feel her love, which melds with the Godly love. The sensation swells like a blossoming rose in my heart. When I open my eyes, the whole room shimmers. My phone vibrates, and I look down at a text message from a friend.

"How is she?" he asks.

I type, "She is going right now."

I look up and see her breathing has stopped. Chills fill my body as I realize my mother, Barbara A. Doolittle, has transitioned into her next adventure.

PART III

ALL IS THEE WHISPERING TO ME HOW TO BE LOVE

No Matter

Recently I disappointed a friend.
We were to meet up and I didn't show.
I apologized but was not forgiven.
So I sit with a heavy heart.

In the face of her anger
my mind has a dozen excuses.
My mother just transitioned.
I haven't slept.
I'm planning a memorial service for 75.
In the end, the Beloved shows me
none of those reasons matter.

Lesley S. King

I can be an imperfect
Friend
Daughter
Sister
Mate
Neighbor
Employee
Driver and
Spiritual student

No matter.

I exist because of God's love for me.

No matter how flawed my lower actions are today
The eternal flame never wavers.

I am It.

All Exists Now

While I am listening to music and washing the morning dishes, my hands warm in the suds, the theme song from *The Mission* comes on my iPhone. My heart lights with the beauty of the flute and base drums.

Suddenly, tears fill my eyes, and within moments I grab a towel and make my way to the couch. The crying comes from deep in my belly and heaves my chest. This song that was my mother's and mine penetrates to the very heart of my missing her.

"How can face life without her?" I ask the Beloved.

My sobs quiet and my body fills with calm, the sadness passing like a wave, my heart clean and open.

I see that with the Lover my mother is right here, so she is not gone at all.

The very best of her is present in every moment.

I get up off the couch and return to my dishes, glowing with the morning sun.

Soul's Great Gear

I've always appreciated good gear.

It's a fabulous feeling to be among the peaks of the Rockies or the shores of Alaska's islands with the wind blowing and sleet pelting, and yet be completely warm and comfortable.

Our lower bodies—physical, emotional, mental—are the great gear for our soul. They take the hit of the elements, while soul sits safely ensconced, unharmed, unwavering.

The problem arises when we think our furry fleece hat, GORE-TEX jacket, and waterproof boots are us.

In truth, we are soul.

As we open to this reality, the lower layers fade in importance, until we fully embody the love that we are.

Be the Harmony You Want to See in the World

I sit in court on the witness stand while the opposition tries to discredit me.

"In 2008, did you misread the well meter by thousands of gallons?" the opposing attorney asks.

I call on the Beloved. "Yes," I say. My foot bobs and my voice shakes, but I sit tall and hold my head high.

"In 2009, did you make a math error in your calculations?"

"Yes."

Believe it or not, our well association is back in court. After our victory, Dee filed an appeal to the district court, and so here we are.

The hearing continues as the opposition offers up my mistakes over the past five years. They are not many, but Dee's attorney, a weak-chinned man with beard stubble, casts them in the darkest light possible.

Fortunately, our attorney has coached me. I am not to defend myself, nor even try to explain. Any explaining can come when he questions me later. Then I may tell how, at the time, I owned and corrected each error.

Still, I am aware of the reflection—how in life we are continuously bombarded by our shortcomings. My tendency has been to fight, to defend myself. But I now know that is not necessary. The love is within me, and so when I make mistakes, I correct them as best I can, apologize, and move on. I am forgiven.

I am love.

Even as I sit in the witness box, drilled with queries, I feel the flame of my true self burning within. This is a power that can never be doused. It never waivers, and when I focus within, it only burns brighter.

This courtroom is larger than the Santa Fe Magistrate Court, with high ceilings, microphones we speak into, and an overhead projector that casts the exhibits onto screens scattered about. The judge wears a robe and sits on a dais—his expectations loftier and more precise. But my goal is the same: it matters not whether we win or lose—I must stay centered in the Master.

As I leave the witness stand, I walk in a cadence with my mantra, which I chant inside, feeling the love that I am.

The opposing side takes the stand to tell her story. Dee says that all of the conflict has arisen because of poor water pressure in her house. Due to this, and a litany of other reasons, she has refused to pay for well repairs and expenses over the past five years. We have offered to help remedy her water problems, but she will not cooperate.

Her accusations are wild and unreasonable. She says we use magnets to alter her meter readings. And she still insists that we vandalized her property by throwing mice in her bathtub and rats on her land.

As I sit listening, I remember that this well and the water that flows from it symbolize love. The ongoing fight reflects my own inner war. Each part of me believes that it has to battle to get its portion of the elixir. My mind, my emotions, my physical body, each attempt to steal and hold onto the power—the love—what little is available from the material well.

A great shift comes, though, as I truly turn my seeking inward toward divine love. Like a tsunami, it drenches me. I float and dive down into its wonder. I swirl, tumble, and marvel at its sweet bubbles and cool rivulets running across my skin.

Best of all, when I remain in the Ocean of Love and Mercy, my mind, emotions and physical body quiet. They stop fighting and surrender. What previously were many parts, become one great whole of love.

A gentle smile stretches across my face.

After seven hours of testimony, the judge sets forth his ruling. He sides with us on major points, but doesn't declare a winner. Instead he asks us to take three weeks to attempt to settle the case.

As we pack up our files, my mind is frustrated. It wants victory. But when we leave the court, I glimpse the blue Sangre de Cristo Mountains out the window, shadowed by stunning thunderheads, and see reason in the judge's determination.

A win would have gotten us the money we are owed, but we would remain in the same quandary, with a party who refuses to cooperate. The judge's order directs Dee to engage with the whole, to attempt to find a solution, something she has been unwilling to do.

I know my role in this quest for harmony. It is not to try to make the various parts come together—that is mind's solution, and all these years it has failed.

My job is to love my Master, to swim in the great ocean from which harmony births. I do my best to actuate love in the world. But what manifests is not my call, nor is it my business. All in the material world is an effect of my higher causes.

Truly, with the Beloved, I can be happy even as this well conflict plays out in the lower worlds.

Rather than fight for love, my task is to surrender yet more to it.

Dive Soul-First into Love

In every moment
I suspend thought
image the Master
and act from that vibration of pure love
knowing that I am It.

Streaming Love

I stand within my late mother's empty bedroom, where the scent of mildew taints the air. I note the empty wall where the TV hung and the four indentations on the carpet where the bed sat. Only a few piles of miscellaneous things clutter the floor. Most absent is the beautiful being with whom I shared my life.

Suddenly a stab of pain comes to my heart as I realize I gave away the one possession that in the past few years brought us the most jubilance.

Every Sunday I would come to her home and make us brunch. While we ate fried eggs and roasted potatoes, we would talk about relationships, travel, and adventure.

By this time she was fairly confined to bed. And so, the outer adventures we shared—traveling the world and especially New Mexico, visiting ruins and markets, scuba diving and bird watching—transformed to a quieter one: watching movies.

Every week we would lie in her big bed in front of her massive Sony HDTV and laugh, cry, tremble with fear, or swoon with romance. Afterward we would talk of the movie, how it touched us, saddened us, inspired us.

In the weeks following her passing, I became the distributor of her possessions. A bit overwhelmed by the task, I simply did the best I could. When my siblings and cousins arrived from distant towns, I said, "Help yourself" to many of her things. They respectfully did.

But now as I stand in her bedroom, I realize that without even considering, I let go of my mother's entire DVD library. It was a carefully selected set of some fifty movies that she cherished, and that included many of our mutual favorites such as *Good Will Hunting, Forrest Gump*, and *Chicago*. I have no idea who claimed them—at this moment they could be in Austin, Denver, or Dallas.

I sit down on the dusty carpet and cry. The one movie I most lament giving up is *The Mission*. It was our all-time favorite. Starring Robert De Niro and Jeremy Irons, it most matched our mutual criteria of epic scenery, drama, music, and, especially, heart. We watched it many times and discussed it many more. On our travels, we listened to the soundtrack, marveling at the artistry of composer Ennio Morricone.

The loss of it so hurts, because it seems to embody our life together. It was a life of extremes. My mother was a master creator, who during my childhood manifested a sprawling New Mexico ranch where people convened for elaborate feasts, hot-air balloon rides, and cattle drives amid a stunning setting of green meadows and arching willow trees. Meanwhile, her passion for partying took her down dark roads that I often traveled with her, mopping up the aftermath.

As I built my travel-writing career, she often joined in. When I worked in Asia, she met me in Bali, and we traveled back around the world, through Thailand, Nepal, India, Kenya, and Egypt. In New Mexico, she often supplied the enthusiasm for my monthly King of the Road trips I wrote about in *New Mexico Magazine.* She was always happy to explore the state's little towns, even when I left her all day in the No Scum Allowed Saloon.

During those years, she endured my worst fears, my impatience and anger, and yet loved me entirely. Together we lived a thousand epic movies and found, in our own unconditional love, a happily-ever-after.

Shadowed by a cloud of sadness, I leave my mother's house. And in subsequent days, whenever I think of the loss of that library, and especially *The Mission,* my heart hurts so deeply I nearly double over.

I release it to the Beloved, again and again.

One day, clarity comes. I recognize that *The Mission* itself is a small loss. I can likely stream the video online, as I probably can any of the others. And then this truth comes: In a similar way, I can still "stream" my mother's presence into my life—her love, courage, ability to live expansively and generously, and most memorably, her laughter, which I heard so often.

All of these qualities exist within me. When I center in the Beloved, they are here completely. The loss of the movie fades, replaced by a sense of love available to me any moment I ask.

Weeks later, back in her bedroom, I set about the task of sorting through those last miscellaneous piles. Into a keeper box go old photographs and journals, while into a trash bin go dog toys and cassette tapes. I lift a tattered ream of paper and find underneath a single video. The back has swirls of darkness and blue. My heartbeat accelerates and tears well in my eyes.

I flip the video box over, and there it is: *The Mission.*

The Stunning Higher View

Sitting in my car, I don my sun hat and lace up my boots in preparation for a morning hike. My phone rings, and when I answer, I hear the voice of the attorney for our well association. He sounds earnest as he asks how I am.

My heartbeat accelerates, assuming he is calling to report the judge's final ruling in our case. Although I assume we will win, I know better than to be certain of anything in the material world. It is such an unsteady, mercurial place that one can never rely on it. Because of this, in the past weeks, whenever the idea of this judgment has entered my consciousness, I have released all outcomes to the Master.

Our association did, as the judge directed us, try to settle with Dee. But she didn't respond and so, all is left to the highest court in the land—the Santa Fe District Court.

Out the windshield of my car, finches chirp and leap among branches of an apricot tree. Cumulus clouds skate across an azure sky. Truly, I sense, the outcome matters not. What matters is my willingness to courageously walk through any experience, while holding the Beloved's hand. I know that all arises in me, of me, and for me. All contributes to my ascension in spirit.

The attorney's emotionless voice does give me pause. We must have lost, I think. I swallow and take hold of the steering wheel.

"You won," he says.

"Really?"

"Yes, the judge did award Dee the cost of a few repair bills, but on all counts, he sided with you."

As well, the attorney informs me, Dee is to pay the legal bills, which exceed the amount she owes us fivefold.

I smile and the light shining in my car window takes on a golden hue. I thank him and head out on my walk.

As I traverse a piñon forest bordering a golf course, I feel the mind take hold of this. It is elated, feels righteous. It wants me to jump up and down with glee over victory in a battle that has lasted some six years, taken hundreds of hours and thousands of dollars, and caused countless sleepless nights and furious tears.

I call on the Master and hold that response at bay. I realize that the victory is not in the ruling but in what I do with it in this moment. My attachment to my house, money, and time caused this very karma. I had to walk through the experience in order to be where I am today, hiking among the beauty of an unshakable love that is neither for nor against any outcome, but instead exists in the paradise of the divine now.

On the trail I round a bend and suddenly come into a view across acres of green grass capped in the distance by the stunning blue of the Jemez Mountains. Viewing from this higher vantage, I see yet more. This court case reflects my willingness to stand up to my material mind.

Much of my life has been dedicated to earning money, success, and prestige in my work, even at the cost of my own well-being. Now my own high court rules instead for values of love and truth. My focus is much more directed toward kindness to myself and others, trusting that the Beloved will take care of my sustenance. This is cause for celebration.

I also assume that the struggle with this soul, Dee, may not be over. If subtle levels of karma persist, the Master will take me through them, and I am willing because I know the outcome will only open me yet more to the love that I truly am.

Win or lose, when I remain in the arms of the Beloved, I am always victorious.

With that thought, I leap in the air and yell, "Yes!"

The Pure House

I must caulk around the lintels
patch the roof
paint the walls
shim the doors
fix the leaky faucet
confront the pack rats.

I hold my breath
the geyser of impatience
ready to spew.
I must get it done
so I can have peace.

Lesley S. King

The Beloved draws me up
into His arms,
whispers in my ear,
"Sit on the porch, dear one.
Drink tea and eat cherries.
Gaze out at the purple storm clouds.
Love Me,
while I fix the house."

Live Your Dream

I walk room to room with a willowy woman who cherishes her cats. As we look over the garage, she talks of them, the ones from her past, who have died, and the two in her present life, who remind her of the past ones. She ticks off their names, so many cats that I grow confused.

My pulse accelerates with a desire to sell, to convince her that she must rent this house that my mother bequeathed me, and that I have spent thousands of dollars renovating over the past few months.

Our shoes clap across the new maple floors as we make our way through the hall into the master bedroom. There, where the air smells of fresh paint, she rushes to examine the walk-in closet. A smile stretches across her face as she examines the clothing rods and shelves where she might store her belongings.

Her enthusiasm eases my heart. Maybe, just maybe, she will want to live in this house. Then my plan will be in motion.

My ambition to have more time with my True Love, rather than working so hard, will be realized.

We meander back to the front entrance and stand in a ray of sun shining in through the open door. "I adore it," she says. "It's so peaceful."

I give her a rental application, which she agrees to fill out and return to me. When she leaves, I feel light, as though my dream is within reach.

In the next few hours, I show the house to two more possible tenants, and they like it too. I sense I'm on my way.

I sleep a restless night. When I awaken, I call on the Beloved and check my email and voice mail, but find no messages. Days pass without a word, and slowly the possibility dawns on me that my whole scheme might not work. The voice of doom speaks: "No one will rent it. It will remain a vacant space, sucking resources in the form of heat, electricity, and taxes."

The dream of more time with the Master—dead.

As I complete final repairs on the house, pay bills, grocery shop, and take my daily walk, those prospective tenants arise again and again in my consciousness. Each time they do, I ask for guidance and release them, coming back into the now.

As I detach and reattach, I become like Elvis in my bed at night—all shaking hips and wiggling feet to the tune of my discomfort. I see my ego that wants so badly to do this right, to get the perfect tenant, to have an easier life. It holds on so tightly to these things that all grinds to a halt: no calls come from anyone.

One morning in my spiritual practice, a truth emerges: I don't rely on rental income. I am supported by the True Sustainer. I am all sustenance.

I get up and make my way through the day, still a bit wobbly, but with more sure footing. I show the house to a young couple with a newly adopted child, two dogs, and a cat—with so many pets, not ideal tenants, but possibilities.

With each showing I become clearer about what would serve me: a tenant who is financially responsible, upbeat, with no pets, maybe. I feel myself reclaim my power.

Then, as I take my evening walk and gaze out across an expanse of piñon forest, I begin laughing. I laugh until tears fill my eyes. I realize that this house is not my source. The life I seek, I am already living. I have been for months.

It is a life in which I wake with the Master Power's name on my lips. I sip the tea of Its strength, savor the food of Its kindness. During my daily walks, I breathe the sweet scent of Its breath, and as I work at my computer keyboard, I tap the rhythm of Its heartbeat.

I need not wait for this life I long to live. Instead I simply live it. That is how it appears before me in the material world.

The outer life reflects the inner.

And the woman with the cats?

She called to say she wanted to rent the house, but the Omniscient Realtor urged me to decline her. I now have some better options.

The Beloved's House

I call on the Friend and easily sign my name on an agreement to lease out my late mother's house. While the new tenants sign, I glance at the kitchen where we stand, its white counter and clean paint. Though darkness settles out the window, here all is bright.

But later, back at my own house, as I eat my chicken and green-bean dinner, a tear drips down my cheek. I don't know why.

Later still, in the night, images come of times in that house.

It's a kaleidoscope of kindness, anger, patience, impatience, happiness, sadness, forgiveness, and love—some twenty-five years between those walls with my mother.

The time I scalded the kitchen counter with a hot pan, only to lift the pan to the sink where it chipped the porcelain, only to transfer it to the floor where it burned the linoleum, all in less than a minute.

And my mother forgave me.

The time when Mom and I studied our scuba at the dining room table, trepidatiously preparing for our final checkout dive at the crystalline Blue Hole, a sinkhole in eastern New Mexico.

An afternoon of trying on wigs and head scarves during Mom's chemo, when she'd lost her hair.

Mashing three times the number of potatoes for Thanksgiving in Mom's KitchenAid mixer so that she could have days of leftovers.

The time after her brother, sister, and neighbor died that she took too many pills and passed out on the hall floor.

She lived.

Just hours ago, in the empty house, I gave a key to the new tenants.

They strode through to the living room, discussed where to place the TV, the armoire.

Now, in bed, I'm drawn to a poem by Rumi:
"And God said, 'Why should I not sever from *Myself*
what I want and know is best? All is literally part of Me.
What of existence's perfection and all events therein
can any eyes know…until their mind and all one's
awareness is one with Me?'"

In the quiet of the night, in my own bed, with my cat, Arjuna, cushioned into my legs, I cry deep sobs, and then I see: This house that has been such a part of me is not mine, nor my mother's. It is the Friend's. I own nothing. All is It.

I am no thing. I am the vibration of love.

My mother, that house, have been severed for my own good—like a tree pruned in infancy so all its power can shoot upward to the heavens.

The house was our control center where we planned our adventures. We read guidebooks about Guatemala, Bolivia, and Tuscany.

We fell asleep next to each other in the warm afternoon sun, her oxygen machine pumping a steady heartbeat.

This house was so much more than a house. It was a cocoon where we retreated from the world. It was a time machine where we journeyed to our childhoods and to our futures, a botanical garden where in spring we planted clematis and petunias.

We shed a hundred tears between its walls, laughed a thousand laughs over lost love, sick stomachs, aching limbs, and heartfelt movies—our silly attachment to who we thought we were or should be, or wanted to be, but weren't:

Me a successful writer, friend, mate, daughter.

She a successful mother, grandmother, companion, traveler.

We succeed and fail and fail and fail, and yet we continue to love each other.

And with each parting I would hug her, and with each passing year, we would hold on longer and more tightly, somewhere knowing, understanding, how precious the moments were.

She delighted in talking of our adventures, telling her caregivers, and even strangers, of our game of gin while sitting on the floor of the Seoul train station where Korean men encircled us. They sat on their haunches and hummed and hawed over each of our plays.

Of a flight from Bangkok to Katmandu in which most of the other passengers were small of stature but oddly bulky in their attire. Through whispers on the journey we learned that they were smuggling layers and layers of clothing into Nepal.

Of when I spent days doubled over in pain from amoebic dysentery in Kenya while a riot waged outside our hotel. Mom organized our clandestine escape from the country.

And so I recall how easily I slipped those keys into the tenant's palm.

Keys to a box that appears to hold all of that love inside.

My mother and I both dreamed about houses: grand palaces, little shacks floating in a current, ones with Technicolor gardens, ones with hidden rooms that suddenly appeared.

And now, this dream of a house opens its doors to new inhabitants. And I release it, for I am not in the house, the house is in me.

All those memories, just experiences in the long road of eternity. All the Master.

All love.

All Is a Love Song

How Do I Listen to Thee?

In my morning practice
I listen to the words and sentences
and the whispers in between.

When a challenge arises in my day
I listen to the quiet voice
that helps me find my way.

While I work,
does my computer hum or grind?
I listen.

All In For Love

I note the music playing in my mind.
Is it harp, flute
or heavy metal?
With my mantra
I easily change the station.

I listen to the TV
what the characters say
to my cat and whether she purrs or claws
to the cashier at the grocery checkout
the bumper sticker on the car in front of me.

I listen to my friends
their faces teary-eyed, anguished or beaming
in my presence.

I listen as I eat
read the Beloved's sentences between bites
ponder each as I chew.

On my daily walk
I listen to the ravens caw
relish the way the clouds skid across the blue.

When I sleep
I listen to my dreams
note who I meet
and what they say.

Lesley S. King

When voices yell and berate
I call on the Beloved
to turn them away.

I listen to the silence of eternity.

All is Thee
whispering to me
how to be
Love.

I Am the Child

I pull the little hand-carved Christ figurine from the box and place it in the manger. Next I find Mary and Joseph and set them on either side of the child's tiny crib. As I do this, my heart both tugs downward and rises upward. It's an odd, bitter sweetness on this snowy December evening.

These are the first Christmas decorations I have ever put up in my home of eight years. As I place the three wise men and a shepherd outside the manger, I feel like a kid playing with dolls. I am the master of this little scene, of these delicate hand-carved and painted figures that my parents brought home from Italy when I was a toddler. Now here they are on my entryway table.

Some twenty years ago, this nativity disappeared into an attic, and I only found it after my mother's passing in the spring. Their beauty prompted me to finally decorate my home for Christmas. Although I am not a Christian, I do appreciate the symbolism of the holiday, the birth of the soul child that is happening within each of us as we journey homeward.

In previous years I would decorate and celebrate the holiday at my mother's house. On Christmas Day we would cook brunch and eat at her dining room table adorned with sweet-scented narcissus blossoms. We would drink eggnog and open packages.

After I finish setting up the nativity, I go about my days, blogging, editing, and teaching, but slowly a strange lethargy comes over me. I can't identify it, but sense the Omnipresence wants me to see something.

A health condition I've recently been relieved of returns, which compounds the slow, dark feeling within. I chant my word, read my Master's works, and rest on the couch. These activities lift my spirit, but still I feel as though I am swimming through gray fog.

The weekend comes, and I meet a friend to cross-country ski. With my lassitude, it's a challenge to keep this date, but I do. We drive a snow-packed road to the trailhead where I turn off the motor. We sit in silence for a moment, and then I find myself talking about the nativity, about its grace and the childlike mirth of putting up the figurines.

Suddenly I'm weeping, and my friend, who has been going through her own presolstice lessons, weeps too. For me, it is about saying good-bye to a warm holiday ritual I shared with my mother. Tears drip down my face and into my mouth, the saltiness a healing potion in the silence of this still day under a pumice sky.

After our tears dry, we climb out, put on our skis and head onto a trail dusted with some of the lightest, fastest powder I have ever skied. The shimmering snow clings to the pines and rises in fairy puffs as we brush the branches.

We ski and ski, over hills and through aspen glades. As I speed along the fast parts, I whoop with exuberance at some new freedom that has birthed within. It is a sense of my existence far beyond this physical body—a feeling of peace and love that radiates from me into the cosmos.

In the evening, I again adjust the figurines of the nativity, and as I lift the Christ child, I recognize what a stunning reflection this is. I've used my energy to adorn so many other homes, so many other lives—family, friends, employers. Now, in the ease of loving my Master, I draw that energy in, where it can serve me to claim my own self-realization.

Here on the eve of the solstice, my own soul self births, while the whole scene stands before me in my home.

I am the child born unto Thee.

Land of Eternal Radiance

I trek through a forest of dead imagery
clutch great oaks that wither to dust
search for answers in pools of my tears
to one day breathlessly
meet the One who guides me to
the Land of Eternal Radiance
where the squawking crows quiet
the thunderous pulse slows
and imperatives dissolve into mist
as my being glows.

Dwell in Love

I see a stunning scarlet poppy field backed by blue mountains, the beauty easing my being on a cold Monday morning. But then I look at the source of this image on my Facebook timeline, and my sense of peace turns to ire. "How dare she post this with no credit to the photographer!" I yell to no one but myself.

I get up and pace my home's great room, from the kitchen to the living room where the sun glares in too brightly. The fieriness of these emotions informs me that this is about more than copyright infringement. But what? I release the issue to the Omniscient One and go about my day.

I answer emails and edit a client's essay. I recognize that part of my reaction to this woman's Facebook business page—on which she posts beautiful images she finds on the Internet, always without giving credit—is simply jealousy.

It has taken me many months to build the Facebook page for The Inner Adventure. I put time and energy into creating original content, including hours out shooting photos. How easy it would be to use the very best of the Internet and represent it as my own.

But I also know that's not this woman's intention. She simply has a keen eye for inspiring photographs, and she's using it to good effect. Practically everyone steals images off the Internet these days. Again I release this to the Omniscience.

I log onto Facebook and there find another stunning image from her page. On this one in the comments field, I write, "It would be great to know the source of this, and that person would probably appreciate the credit." It's as neutral a message as I can muster.

In the coming hours, I wait to see if the message kicks back. If it does, it's usually a sign that my own message has a bite.

Still I ask the Beloved to guide me, to show me what this is really about. In the night, while I sleep, the answer begins to come. And in the morning, as I do my reading contemplation, a truth illuminates.

It is I who fails to give credit for the bountiful gifts in my life. Each time I reach to the outer for love, money, health, or recognition, I am denying the true Source.

All comes from the Divine. It is only a trick of the mind that claims responsibility for this magnificent creation that with every breath draws me closer to my true home.

As I enter my day, I'm released from angst toward this beautiful soul and her Facebook page. I receive a message from her explaining where she gets her photographs. Through the innocent reply, I realize she has no idea that she is misusing others' art, and so I briefly explain and direct her to a Facebook page called Photography Copyright that lovingly educates about downloading photographs from the Internet and posting them as your own.

I am able to do this with neutrality because it no longer matters to me what she does. That is her business. On my own photographs, I get the long-overdue nudge to place watermarks—notations with my web address—an easy solution.

Later in the day, I log onto Facebook and see a message from her page saying she will no longer be posting except on her personal page. At first I am struck with a sense of responsibility and sadness at the loss of the beauty of her posts.

In a note back to me, she writes: "I understand it's important to give credit where credit is due." I write back saying that I hope she will continue and simply find a way to give that credit.

A week later I'm closing up the house for the night. I lock the doors and secure the shutters. All is quiet out here in the piñon forest where I live. Suddenly my mind churns about money. It counts days and weeks and years and dollar amounts trying to be sure I will have enough.

I call on the Beloved to stop my mind's grasping.

I suspend into the now, here with my cat, the quiet of the night, and the calming love that flows in upon my simple request.

In the morning as I lie between flannel sheets and listen to the quiet, I recognize the power of that moment. I see that when I let my mind count, calculate, or in any way rely on the outer, I give credit to the mind, as though my sustenance comes from it, from the material world. Instead I can connect with the True Power and move into that spectacular state of knowing that its Infiniteness supplies all, and that I can rely on it always and forever.

With this dawning, I grasp the imperative of dwelling in the love vibration in every moment—since it truly is the Creator.

The Great Oneness

The mind wants to defeat
to decimate
the lower tendencies—
lust
anger
greed
attachment
and vanity.
It wants to win.

Meanwhile,
the Master simply loves
them into submission,
includes them
in the great Oneness
that I am.

No Identity but Love

I'm working peacefully at my computer when I glance out the window and see a six-foot cedar post. I stand to look more closely and come to find that my neighbor is erecting a coyote fence between her property and mine.

Immediately, my mind goes into emergency mode. It's alarmed about the fence placement, which seems to be on my property, not hers. But there's a subtler disturbance within me that I can't quite identify.

Feeling my inner panic, I call on the Beloved. I need this counsel to calm me, to advise me on what to do. I head out on my daily walk. As I make my way down the trail, my mind keeps returning to the fence, and I keep drawing my attention back to my mantra and the image of my Master. Slowly I calm. I can appreciate the cirrus clouds skating across the sky and the chamisa bushes with their downy winter coats.

I come to see that this fence is not a personal strike against me. Ever since our well association won the court case against Dee, she has been erecting fences all around her property. Night and day, sun or rain, she is out there building her fortress.

Arriving back at my house, I walk around the side to get a closer look at the construction. Indeed, Dee has put up five or so main posts and filled in one section with cedar fencing. I hear her working there now.

Behind the blockade, her dog barks. "Good dog," Dee says. "Good dog."

My heart aches with the thought that my neighbor would encourage her dog to bark at me.

Back inside my house, I call the title company to ask what to do. I immediately reach an officer who recommends that I use my property survey to check the measurement from my house to the fence line. I pull out my longest tape measure and head outside. It turns out that the fence is within her property. I simply didn't realize that my house sits so close to her line. Relief washes over me.

As I settle in for the evening, I chop carrots and broccoli for a stir-fry. But I still feel uneasy. It's as though that fence represents my neighbor's hatred of me, and I have trouble reconciling that.

I have always tried so hard to be *nice*. My whole life that is the identity I have most fostered. I stop cooking and look out the window at the sunset, blazing a thousand variations of red, pink, and orange. Suddenly I recognize how limited that identity is. Nice Lesley—how little room there is to act in that matrix.

It is pure ego—a desire to be liked at all cost. The truth is, sometimes I am not nice. I can manifest meanness, thoughtlessness, selfishness, or any number of lower tendencies. Over the years with this neighbor, I have pretty much shown my worst, until recently, when I have come to view her as soul and her combative acts as mere tendencies.

I bring in the Beloved and feel the love encompass my being. This is my true identity. I am not nice Lesley. Instead I am the Divine Power. When I align with it, I become omniscient, omnipotent, and omnipresent. It is the power of all creation. It has the ability to negotiate any situation with compassion.

I see that this experience with my neighbor is not about her and me, fence and property. It is about the unseen forces acting behind these outer manifestations. The opposing force wants to draw me away from the Master. When I stay strong in the love, I realize yet more of my true self.

In subsequent days, the fence construction continues, and I simply let it. I come to see the fence as a beautiful reflection of an important boundary between my higher and lower self. I need not react to, nor fight, nor run from that lower vibration. Instead I can simply let it play out its karma behind its little coyote fence, while I enjoy spring, its chirping birds, cobalt sky, and sun that warms my cheeks.

Above all, I bask in the love that I am.

I Will Always Want You

I will always want you
the Master says to me.

I think back to my mother who didn't
when I was born;
the lovers who did
but then left or I left them;
the employers who did
but paid little, pushed hard
and then disappeared;
the friends who I no longer see,
the wine that once eased
but then hurt my head,
the elaborate feasts
that stole my strength.

Lesley S. King

Even the movies that warmed my heart
one day became dull,
and my dog, Alma, closed her eyes
and didn't reopen them.

I will always want you.
That love, from my true Friend,
with each thought
remembrance
smile
breath and chant
grows wider and broader,
takes me into it and expands me
until I am it
and we are everything,
the oceans and continents
sun, moon, and stars
the winter grass silver in the night
the robin chirping at dawn
the cat curled warm against my side.

I will always want you
is finally true.

How to Live Forever

"I want to be cremated and have my ashes spread near the creek on the Big Tesuque Trail in the Santa Fe Mountains."

On a sunny spring morning, I sit at my dining room table and write this in the will I am preparing. I think little of it. It is but a directive for some day in the future.

Later, while I eat dinner in that same spot, I pause from my chicken and Brussels sprouts, my appetite suddenly gone. A wave of nostalgia washes over me. In my will, I am talking about this body that I have inhabited for a half century.

In those years I have kayaked it over waterfalls, stuffed it with rich food and wine, and entangled it with lovers' limbs. I have nursed it through illness and exalted in its strength.

And yet…

I never thought of it as burning to ashes, vanishing into dust.

I call on the Eternal One, and the sadness eases but still lingers. My appetite returns enough so I can finish dinner and go to bed.

The next morning, I'm reading a contemplation note in my sauna, the warmth seeping into my bones. Suddenly the light blinks off and the hum of the infrared emitters quiets. Is it a power outage, I wonder? I climb out, tiptoe across the cold concrete, and see that my surge protector has died. I attach the plug to the wall socket and resume my practice, the power full on.

Later in the morning in my office, I click on a YouTube video called *The Thunderbolts of the Gods.* Through vivid images of the cosmos and interviews with scientists, the documentary presents recent findings in astronomy. Apparently Einstein's theory that the universe is held together through gravity is being replaced with a theory that electricity instead infuses the universe. The science is beyond my comprehension, but I do get a sense that the Master is showing me something profound, though I'm not sure what.

Later in the day, I stand in the guest room of my house, massaging my friend, the air infused with the scent of sesame oil. Each week we exchange massages, a relaxing gift for my body and hers. As Enya croons on the stereo, I rub my fingertips along my friend's arm and down to the palm of her hand. Suddenly, in looking at her fingers, pink and plump with vitality, I see the opposite, the day when life will leave them. They will be dry, crisp, and then dust.

I recall a date I had early in my spiritual quest. My new boyfriend at the time, a premed student, snuck me into the cadaver lab at the University of New Mexico Medical Center. In a state of shock, I wandered around the fluorescent-lit room that smelled of formaldehyde and held twelve bodies, each lying faceup on a gurney. I finally stopped next to an old woman. Her body lay thin, gray, lifeless, but her irises retained a mind-blowing sapphire hue. Looking into those marbles, I knew without a doubt that a body is only a temporary home for something much larger.

As I massage down my friend's legs and feet and run my thumb between her toes, the Beloved takes me on a trip. I see the Current that fills this body is like the electricity that powers my sauna. Except the Divine Current never blinks, never ceases. It is an eternal charge running through all life—enlivening the whole universe—including me.

I look at my hands as they knead my friend's muscles and recognize that this body, this temple where I reside for a time, will surely go, but I won't. I am the everlasting Current, and the very basis of that Current is love.

When I finish the massage, I move quietly to my living room. My feet dance across the floor, my heart so light I feel as though I am flying. I look out the window where the piñon trees, the blue jays, and the sky with wispy spring clouds seem to shimmer with light. Today's trials—health concerns, tension with my neighbor, uncertainty about the future—are but blips on the screen of my eternal radar. I can overcome anything. But most of all, I can be my true spiritual self.

Harmony of the Whole

On my morning walk through the piñon forest surrounding my house, I suddenly note a sharp pain in my knee. It is on the inner part just below my kneecap. I ask for the Beloved's help and get the sense to adjust my gait so that I am not so forward. The pain eases enough so I can enjoy the stunningly clear sky and the mountain bluebirds tripping across the treetops.

But as I make my way home, the pain persists, and in the coming days, it flares up now and then. It is especially notable at night before I fall asleep, when my body is tired.

Days later, as once again my walk turns challenging because of the pain, I face the many subtle fears surrounding the experience. As I limp along, I see I am afraid of the cost of going to a doctor to get x-rays, and possibly surgery. Although I have health insurance, my deductible is in the thousands. And then the deeper fear yet, that this could somehow take away my most treasured activities: walking, hiking, skiing, cycling, and swimming.

My mind wants to figure out the cause. Daily I do alignment exercises to keep my body fit and flexible, so why is this happening? Did I injure the knee when I fell on the Na Pali Coast Trail in Kauai? Am I walking improperly? Certainly a root cause is an old ski injury, but why is it flaring up now?

I don't let my mind dwell on this—for I know that if I do, I create more of it. Instead I release all and make my way home.

Before bed I ask on the inner for guidance. The next day I call a health hotline. The nurse goes through the standard triage and determines that nothing serious is happening, which eases my mind. Slowly as I walk, pet Arjuna, and cook my meals, I become willing—to go to a knee doc, to even lose those activities so dear to me. What is truly important, I see, is my connection to the Divine.

A longtime friend comes to visit from Albuquerque. We talk, eat lunch, and head out for a walk. So released am I from my knee situation I don't even mention it to her, though I feel some pain as we make our way over hills and through arroyos.

I ask her about shoes for walking. Should I have more support or less? She explains that it depends on the strength of my arches. Back at my house, she—a physical therapist—asks to look at my feet to help determine the best kind of shoes.

When I roll up my pant leg, she immediately sees my knee and says, "What's going on there?" She points out the bone spur—a bump on the inside, the sight of which has been troubling me. Then she has me show her how I walk.

She mimics it for me, and I see that I walk as though my right buttock is frozen. The movement looks a bit like an armadillo's gait. She shows me a different way and then gives me three exercises to do to waken the muscles.

In the coming days, I do the exercises and practice walking, using that hip. What's amazing is I find that in swimming too I haven't been using the full force of that leg but instead have relied more on the flutter of my calf. When I walk and swim, I now feel the power of my gluteus maximus and thigh. Meanwhile, my shoulders and chest seem to awaken too, so my whole body participates in these activities.

When I walk like this, I feel no pain. All activity seems to emanate from my immensely strong core.

I'm rounding the last corner of my walk, a slow rise that peaks with a spectacular view of the Sangre de Cristo Mountains. Suddenly I feel the power of all my body parts working together.

And I see the parallel inside. When I am not centered in my true self, each part of me vies for dominance. The physical body wants its pleasures fulfilled. The emotions desire safety and happiness. The mind demands to rule over all, with its agenda of excitement and engagement. It is like an orchestra in which each part thinks it's the soloist. But when soul takes the ascendant, all bodies fall into line, all help to harmonize and ascend.

My hips roll, my shoulders shift so my arms can swing with freedom. Yes, this is the harmony of the whole, played in the key of love.

When Seasons Collide

Fluttery white flakes
caress chive blossoms.
Piñon smoke
licks baby grass.
Winter unites with spring
birthing love.

The Lover Appears

At dawn I sit on the porch
with my Lover.
We sip licorice tea
and listen to finches chirp
and doves coo.

During the day
we work together—
sweep the floors
cook fennel with snow peas,
even the mundane tasks
joyful because we are together.

All In For Love

We collaborate on creative projects
like this poem.
I listen as the Lover
flows the words through my pen.

And then we spontaneously
waltz around the great room
to the silent Sound.

I had dreamed of
a love such as this,
a mate to share my days,
who is willing to face challenge
without cruelty,
to leap off the great cliff
certain we will soar.

Someone who cares
no matter
the state of my physical body
no matter
the shakiness of my emotions
or the agitation of my thoughts.

I had given up hope
content in my solitude
until one day
the Lover appeared.

Lesley S. King

And I realized this Presence
had been here all along.

It was like a too-small apartment:
One day you open a door
and a whole new room appears.

Or that sweater you desired,
only to find
it was already in your closet.

Now that I know the Lover is here
we never part.
Like any new companionship
we can't get enough of each other
talking into the late hours
about nothing and everything.

And then we sleep
spooned into one another
so close that I realize
the Lover is me.

Life with a True Master

I awaken after a long night's sleep, go to the kitchen to heat some water, and sit down in a chair to do my spiritual practice. The morning is quiet, with only the sound of dew dripping from the roof. I cherish the ritual that always fills me with merriment, which I then bring into my day and give of freely.

It hasn't always been this way.

When I started on the MasterPath, I used to meditate. Each morning I would read some spiritual writing and then sit for a half hour or so attempting to quiet my mind. Occasionally, I would reach a state of release, but more often the time felt like a fight, as my mind insisted on thinking, calculating, and trying.

This is one of many things I surrendered when I gained the guidance of a true spiritual master. My life at the time was very busy—my writing work kept me running from deadline to deadline. When I wasn't working or traveling for work, I kayaked, biked, ran, and skied with friends. As well, I traveled on weekends to my family's ranch to see them and to help with the cattle and horses. It seemed like a normal life, and it was, though it allowed little time for introspection.

My relationship with the man who brought me to my knees continued, though now with the Path, I had more tools. When my boyfriend wouldn't call me, I would detach and instead focus on the love that my Master embodies. This allowed me to be in the now, to focus on my own life and live it fully. One day, I simply didn't care whether my boyfriend called or not. Inevitably, moments after that release, he did call.

After many months of this, I grew to be more neutral about the whole relationship. I always knew that the love was within, but I'd never really felt it, and with the help of the Master, I did. It is a sense of peace centered at my third eye, the spot between my two eyes and a little above. That tranquil ardor then radiates through my entire being. Once I experienced this inner love, my boyfriend decided to join the MasterPath too.

Shortly after that, he ended our relationship in order to be free to date other women. It was painful for me, but I could see the perfection. The Master released me from the challenge of the relationship and released my boyfriend to explore the freedom that he seemed to always want.

Meanwhile, I came to understand more about spirituality. Through reading the MasterPath literature, I began to see that the journey of soul is a journey through the body. In the body the Divine has placed a map to our true home. We climb through the chakras; each ascending one represents a more refined vibration.

In this journey from the elimination chakra through the reproductive, the heart and throat, we master the placement of our attention, so that nothing can pull us away from our devotion. Once we do, we graduate to yet more subtle versions of the same. As I made this journey with my Master, my whole viewpoint about life shifted. Rather than challenging experiences seeming completely random—and mostly harmful to me—I began to see the beauty of each.

Here's how this manifested:

- In my early days on the MasterPath, I worked through residual desire to have a child. The Beloved graced me with a vicarious motherhood experience that showed me that the true child I am to nurture is my soul.
- Next, I found a mate who really wanted a relationship. He was spiritual, beautiful, and kind. But even with all this, over time our admiration dissipated. Through this I really understood that my one true love is my Beloved inner self.
- I had great success with work, saw my writing recognized and celebrated, only to realize how little true satisfaction that most-coveted of goals brought me. This showed me that my truest creation is my spiritual life, my love for the Master, and my quest for self and God realization.

With the Master's guidance, I continue to climb through the chakras, each opening me to yet more love. The mind needs something to love beyond itself, and that is the beauty of having a true Master. A devotee loves one's Master, who is the embodiment of God—and this God is within the devotee—within me.

I complete my morning reading with a smile on my face. My body and mind are calm and full of rapture. I am in love, with my Master, my true self, and all of life. I know that all is God, that every experience is here to show me that I am the very essence of the Divine—I am all strength, compassion, and love. Most importantly, I can live these qualities and thus give to others.

Sounderella

I always wanted someone
to steal me away
on a grand sailboat
to a tropical isle,
with palms and a turquoise bay,
or in a plane
over lofty peaks
to wildflower meadows
where butterflies play.

I longed to leave my desert
the pain of this anvil heart
the boredom of my heavy-metal playlist,
find a new start.

Lesley S. King

One day the Beloved arrives
on a white stallion,
His entrance quieting the din.
He scoops me up
behind him on the saddle
and we ride toward home,
inward and yet farther in.

We skirt thunderheads
leap from cirrus to cirrus
and higher yet
into the pure empty blue
where the Music plays silently
a profound melody of freedom
a heart one with the Hu.*

We canter and canter
until He passes the reins
from His palm
to my own
and I realize
this is my horse,
my ride
and I
am home.

*In the mystical teachings, the Divine Presence is given form as audible vibration.

The Highest Quest

*Now is the time to understand that all your ideas of
right and wrong were just a child's training wheels,
to be laid aside when you could finally
live with veracity and courage.*

—Hafiz

I wake to lemony dawn light peeking around my bedroom blinds. My heart jumps with some sense that I must leap up, meet a deadline, and pack my bags to head off on a work trip, but I call on the Master and my pulse settles. That is no longer my life.

I rise, do my spiritual practice, and make chai tea. I stretch, eat breakfast, and sit down to write. What I write is the purest truth I've ever written. It is as much about God as is possible in this part of my journey, and my heart swells over the fact that this is what I get to do each day.

In the three years since that Acoma pot evaporated between my fingers, my life has fallen apart and come back together, like a puzzle with pieces strewn all about, each slowly finding its place.

My work that once hurt me to the point of illness now soothes me as I channel the love that flows through. Since I rely on the Master for my sustenance, I no longer spend my days striving to get money. Instead my focus is on serving, giving love, and the money comes from the true Source.

Just a few years ago, I couldn't have imagined that my mother would pass. She, though not very mobile, still had a strong constitution. And yet, her time had come. Her departure left me with property through which the Master channels money to help fund my life. The many challenges I faced in caring for and loving my mother—her attachment to alcohol, my attachment to her—have dissipated, and yet I can still feel the love between us whenever I turn inward.

The conflict with my neighbor has not resolved completely, but our community did stand up to her bully vibration and won. Each time I am asked to enter the arena with her, I do so with yet more neutrality, and that is the true victory. These lessons come slowly, sometimes day after day of being "in" them, working through the challenges they present. Most days I am stunned by the beauty of this divine system, every note in the symphony perfectly orchestrated to bring us home.

What I most treasure now is that I spend my days with the Master. After my morning practice and writing, I do my best to continue to luxuriate in the peaceful turquoise sea. I consult with writing students, hire a plumber, buy a new washer for my rental, and have lunch with friends who like to talk of the Master. I walk, swim, and ride my bike to the cadence of Its steady tide.

Certainly I get pulled out of my centered state, and then I know I must look closely at what stole my attention. I do, and when I bring in the Master, these encounters dissipate and unveil a whole new level of love. This is the inner adventure, a constant challenge, more intense than any job or sport. It is the highest quest, in which one comes to realize the divine self.

ABOUT THE AUTHOR

Lesley S. King grew up on a ranch in northern New Mexico. From a young age, she knew she wanted to write and to pursue truth. She majored in journalism in college and creative writing in graduate school. For eight years she taught college English, until she found the courage to begin writing professionally. Her career quickly gathered momentum and soon she was writing for the *New York Times,* the Frommer's and Dummies travel guides, *Audubon* magazine, and United Airlines *Hemispheres Magazine*. For eight years she wrote, photographed, and videotaped stories for her King of the Road column in *New Mexico Magazine*. In 1997, she came under the tutelage of spiritual Master Sri Gary Olsen. Since then she has devoted her life to the inner journey. She is author of many travel guidebooks and a novel, *The Baby Pact,* and she blogs at The Inner Adventure.

www.lesleysking.com

Made in the USA
San Bernardino, CA
11 August 2016